# THE INTERNET
# MADE EASY

Find What You've Been Searching For

## By James Bernstein

GW00993625

Bernstein, James
The Internet Made Easy
Book 9 in the Computers Made Easy series

For more information on reproducing sections of this book or sales of this book,
go to www.onlinecomputertips.com

# Contents

# Introduction

With everything being "connected" these days, we tend to rely on online services more and more just to get by with the basics such as paying bills, buying movie tickets, and communicating with friends and family. And if you are not online in one way or another, you might find yourself not being able to do things such as applying for a job or getting the instruction manual for your new TV.

Keep in mind that if you prefer to do things the old-fashioned way (while you still can) that is fine, but it's always a good idea to get yourself acquainted with current ways of doing things for when the time comes where it's the only way to do them. Even if you can still do things like go to the ATM for your banking, buy your movie tickets in person, and call your friends on the phone, it doesn't mean it's not a good idea to start making the transition to the online world, even if it's just for simple web browsing purposes.

The goal of this book is to first get you acquainted with what the Internet is and how it works. Then I will focus on how you can use the Internet to make your life easier and more productive... and even more fun! I will also go over how to keep yourself safe from all of those bad people out there that are looking to take advantage of those who are not so Internet savvy.

This book is not meant to be an advanced book on computing and the complex networking that makes all of the Internet magic happen, but rather was ,put together to give those who may not be the most technical people a leg up on how to increase their online skills and take advantage of all the cool things the Internet has to offer.

So, on that note, grab some coffee and your computer (or other device), and let's see what's out there and what all those millions of other people all over the world are doing!

# Chapter 1 – What is the Internet?

When you hear the word *Internet*, what do you think of? Do you think of things like Google, Amazon, and Facebook, or do you think of things like connecting to your computer at the office from your home computer and sharing a spreadsheet with your coworkers via a web browser? Regardless of what you think of, it's most likely that there is much more you can do on the Internet than you think.

Web browsing is just a part of what you can do with the Internet (even though I will be focusing a lot on this part of it since that's most likely what you will be doing on the Internet yourself). However, since it's such a big part of using the Internet, there are things you should know to make the most of it while keeping you and your personal information safe at the same time.

## History of the Internet
I wanted to begin the discussion of the Internet by going back to where it all began and how it got to where it is today. I will leave out the super technical and boring details and just stick with the interesting facts to give you an overview of how things have progressed throughout the years.

The history of the Internet goes much further back before we all had computers at home and at the office, and even before Microsoft had their Windows operating system. Back in 1969, a team of defense engineers at the University of Los Angeles-California (UCLA) sent the first instant message using a computer to another computer miles away at Stanford University, which paved the way for Arpanet. Arpanet was designed to be a system that would connect computers at the Department of Defense's various locations so that they could share software, information, and storage. From there, everything blew up and the Internet boom started taking shape.

In 1974 the word *Internet* was coined to describe a system of communications and networking protocols designed for managing data transmissions. Then, in 1981, The Computer Science Network is created by the University of Wisconsin-Madison and is used to connect several universities to each other, as well as bringing nationwide attention to the benefits of networking. In 1983 the Domain Naming System (or DNS) was created so we wouldn't have to use the complicated number combinations that pointed to online services and only needed to remember user friendly names that mapped to these numbers.

The real fun began in 1989 with the invention of the Hypertext Markup Language (HTML), which was then used with the newly created web browser in 1990, allowing us to view text and graphics on pages hosted on other computers. This grouping of computers that shared information was then called the "World Wide Web", which you have most likely heard people use. This is where www comes from. In 1993 W3Catalog became the first World Wide Web search engine that indexed the Web and allowed users to find web pages. (I will be going over search engines and web browsers in Chapter 2.)

Here is a listing of some more recent events that you might be interested in:

- 1994 - Jeff Bezos founded Amazon.
- 1998 - Google opened its first office.
- 2004 - Facebook was launched.
- 2006 - Google acquires YouTube.
- 2006 - Twitter is launched.
- 2007 - Smartphones began their quest to dominate the cell phone market.
- 2008 - The Google Chrome web browser was launched.
- 2010 - Instagram is launched.
- 2011 - The number of Internet users reaches 2 billion.
- 2015 - 1 billion users access Facebook on a single day.
- 2015 - Google mobile device searches surpass desktop searches for the first time.
- 2017 - Facebook reaches 2 billion active monthly users.
- 2017 - YouTube reaches 1.5 billion active monthly users.

## How the Internet Works

The Internet is a very complicated network of computers, routers, switches, cabling, and other hardware which I won't be getting into too much detail about, but I think it's a good idea that you know the basics of how it all works. In the next section I will go over some basic networking to hopefully tie it all together. If you don't care about how the Internet works and only care that it works period, then you can skip this section if you want to get to the content that interests you.

The Internet is basically a network of computers (or servers) that are all connected together using connections that are capable of communicating with each other to allow information to pass back and forth through these connections. Back in the beginning these connections were simple, but now they are very complex, and information has to travel through many paths to get where it's going. Just think about if you were visiting a website in another country or continent how far the text and images from that website have to travel to make it to your computer screen and how fast they get there. It's not like there is a cable connecting your computer to the webserver in that country, but rather multiple connections being made to accomplish that task. Figure 1.1 shows the basic idea of your computer at home in the United States connecting to a web server in Europe, and also to one in South America going to two different websites. It's not as simple as the one line between the two showing in the diagram makes it out to be, but rather multiple connections in many locations transferring the data back and forth between the computers.

Figure 1.1

Your computer makes its connection to the webserver by using the public address (IP address) of that web server. These public addresses are assigned to the companies who are hosting the web servers in their datacenters and are unique to that company. But rather than having to know the public IP address, which can look like 46.52.145.212 or worse yet 2001:0db7:85a3:0000:0000:6a2e:0574:7254, we use *DNS* to translate the name of the friendly website name to the web server's IP address. So, when you type the name of the website (such MusicWebsite.com) into your web browser, DNS knows that the IP address for MusicWebsite.com is 46.52.145.212 and sends you to the right place. Then the webserver sends the data you requested (the web page) back to your computer, and you can now view it on your screen. Once that connection between your computer and the webserver is made, it stays connected until it's broken when you do something like close your browser or disconnect from your wireless etc.

**Protocols and Ports**
Since the Internet is used for different purposes, the technology behind the scenes will vary based on what you are trying to accomplish. For the most part, this is taken care of with different protocols, which define rules and conventions for communication between network devices such as your computer and a web server.

One of the most used protocols used on the Internet is the Hypertext Transfer Protocol, or HTTP for short. You might have noticed that the beginning of website addresses in your browser usually have http or even https at the beginning, such as **https**://www.onlinecomputertips.com/. Http defines how messages are formatted and transmitted between computers, and what actions web servers and web browsers should take in response to various commands. Another protocol that is commonly used is FTP, or file transfer protocol, which is used to transfer files from one computer to another over a network or the Internet.

*Ports* are numbers that are used to identify and open each side of a connection between two computers. Port numbers are used to determine which process or application should be used during the communication. There are assigned port numbers for various types of connections such as http (which uses port 80) and https (which uses port 443). FTP uses ports 20 and 21. There is also a large group of unassigned port numbers that can be used for connections that you can customize yourself.

**Simple Networking**
To end this chapter I would like to go over some basic networking concepts and terminology in case you were interested in learning a little about how it all works

in the background. You don't need to know any of this to be a proficient Internet user, so you can read this just for fun (if you are into that kind of thing).

Not all network configurations are the same, but the basic concepts are, so I will discuss the setup you might have at home. In fact, it may be helpful to learn about the equipment you have in order to help diagnose and fix issues with your home Internet service before having to call your provider for help.

There are two common configurations for home Internet access, and I will go over both of them and show you the difference. The first is when you have a separate modem and then a wireless (or Wi-Fi) router (figure 1.2). The modem is what connects to either the phone line or cable outlet depending on your type of service (cable, DSL, fiber etc.) and then gets the Internet connection sent through it.

Then the modem will connect to your wireless router using an Ethernet (network) cable, and then send the Internet signal to it. From there you will connect your wireless devices (such as laptops, tablets, and smartphones) to the router to get their Internet connection. Other devices like desktop computers that might not have wireless capabilities can plug into an Ethernet port on the back of the router for their Internet connection (figure 1.3).

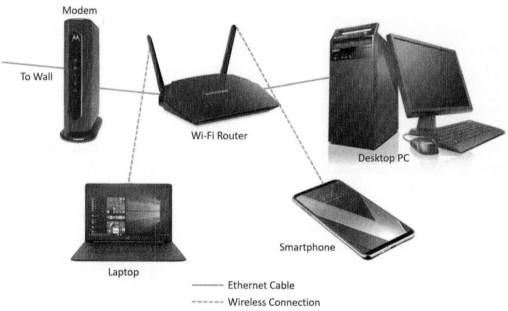

Figure 1.2

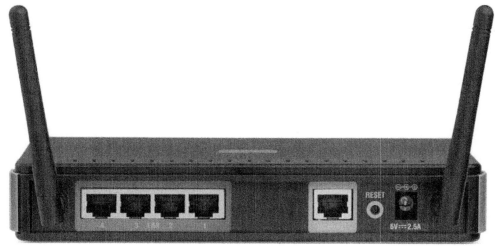

Figure 1.3

Nowadays many modems have built-in wireless capabilities so that you don't need to have a separate wireless router. If you take a look at figure 1.4, you will see that the laptop and smartphone are getting their wireless connection from the modem itself, and that the desktop PC is plugged into an Ethernet port on the back of the modem. This simplifies things and makes it easier to troubleshoot when your connection is lost.

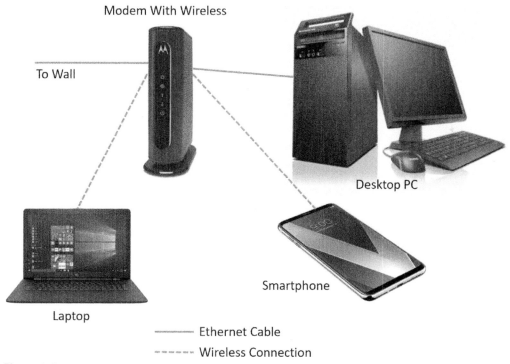

Figure 1.4

Speaking of losing your connection, if that does happen it's common to reset the power to your modem and give it a few minutes to see if that clears things up before calling your provider (because they are going to have you do that anyway!). If you have a router, then you can try to reboot that first to see if that fixes it. If not, then reboot the modem, wait for all the lights to come back on, then reboot the router again. It's also a good idea to reboot your computer after that since the router gets its settings from the modem and your computer gets its settings from the router.

 Just because your wireless device is connected to your wireless connection doesn't mean you will be getting an Internet connection since connecting to your Wi-Fi hotspot and the hotspot connecting to the Internet are two different pieces to the puzzle.

One other thing I want to mention about wireless connections is what is known as the SSID, or Service Set Identifier. This is the name of your wireless connection that your wireless devices connect to. If you take a look at figure 1.5 it shows the available wireless connections in my area that my computer is picking up. Just because they are listed there doesn't mean I can connect to them and use them, and the ones I don't recognize are most likely from offices in the surrounding area. Also, notice how they say *secured* under the name. That is because they are password protected, which hopefully yours is as well. If not, then that means other people who are in range of your signal can connect and use your Internet connection, and you are responsible for what they do with it!

Figure 1.5

# Chapter 2 – Web Browsers and Search Engines

If you plan on being a regular "web surfer" and utilizing the Internet on a regular basis, then that will require you to use a web browser to do so because without one then you are not going to get too far... if anywhere at all. And if you are going to perform searches on the Internet, then you will need to use a search engine for that. One common mistake many people make is confusing a web browser with a search engine or thinking they are both the same thing when in fact they are not at all.

## What's the Difference?

The difference between and web browser and a search engine boils down to that a web browser is software installed on your computer or mobile device (smartphone, tablet etc.) used to display web pages, while a search engine is a website that you use WITHIN a web browser to perform searches. So technically you are using a search engine website to search for other websites by using web browser software.

This may sound a little redundant, but after you read the next sections that go into details about web browsers and search engines, things will make a little more sense. Knowing the difference between the two will make you a more efficient web user and will also allow you to experiment with different browsers and search engines to find the ones that work best for you. And yes, there are more than one of each!

## Web Browsers

Like I mentioned in the last section, web browsers are software installed on your computer or mobile device that are used to display the text and images from websites. Most computers and other devices come with one or more already installed, but you can install others and use more than one at a time. For example, Windows 10 computers will come preinstalled with the Edge web browser and Apple computers (and iPhones) will come preinstalled with the Safari web browser. When reading this information, keep in mind that the process for various tasks will vary between browsers and it's impossible to show every process for every browser. Here is a listing of the more commonly used web browsers:

- Google Chrome
- Microsoft Edge
- Microsoft Internet Explorer (now replaced with Edge)

- Safari
- Mozilla Firefox

Like I mentioned before, you can install more than one web browser on your computer so you can try them out and find the one that you like best. For the most part, they all operate in a similar fashion, but they will vary in ways such as how the menu items are laid out, how bookmarks are used, and also how they perform. Plus they are all customizable to some degree so you can tweak them to your liking.

 Different web browsers will perform differently depending on what you are using them on. For example, Google Chrome might perform better on an Android smartphone compared to an iPhone since Google makes the Android operating system.

Figure 2.1 shows an example of the Microsoft Edge web browser that comes installed with Windows 10. As you can see, there are a lot of components that make up a web browser, but that doesn't mean you should be intimidated by them.

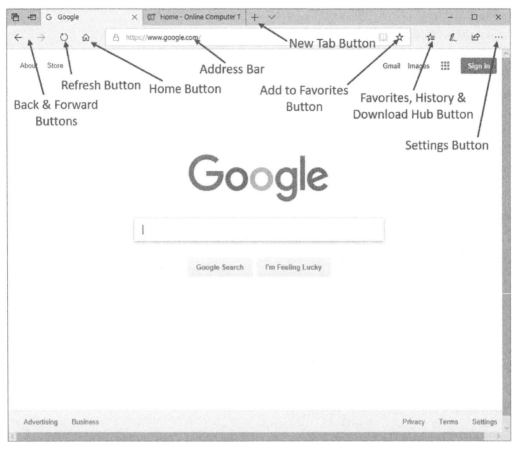

Figure 2.1

Now I will go over each of the main areas of a typical web browser. Keep in mind that they can vary a bit from browser to browser.

- **Address Bar** – This is where you type in the website addresses you want to go to if you prefer to do that rather than do a search for the site. (I will discuss addresses some more later in the chapter.)

- **New Tab Button** – All modern browsers allow you to have multiple website pages open within one web browser session. Simply click the new tab button and it will open up another page that you can use to browse to another site while leaving your other pages open. (I will go into tabs later in this chapter.)

- **Add to Favorites Button** – Use this button to add websites that you are on to your favorites so you can easily find them later and go back to them. Favorites are also known as bookmarks.

- **Home Button** – Clicking on this button will take you to your home page, which can be customized to whatever you want it to be.

- **Refresh Button** – If you want to reload the web page you are on to check for updates or in case it doesn't seem to be responding, you can press this button. (F5 on the keyboard will do the same thing.)

- **Back & Forward Buttons** – You can cycle backward and forwards through all the pages you have been to within a certain tab with these buttons.

- **Favorites, History & Download** – If you go here you can view your favorites or bookmarked sites, go through your browsing history, and also look at your downloaded files.

- **Settings Button** – This is where you can configure and customize your browser to suit your needs. You can also do things like set your default home page, clear your history, and check out your saved passwords.

Now that you can see the main components of a typical web browser, you can try out some other browsers to see how they work and find the one that works best for you.

I like to stick with one web browser because once you start having it save things (like your information, bookmarks, and passwords) it will make things more complicated when switching back and forth between other browsers since one will most likely have information stored that another won't.

To install another web browser simply go to the website for that browser, download the installation file, and install it like you would any other program on your computer. For mobile devices you can go to the App Store (Apple) or Play Store (Android) and install a new browser from there.

Once you find the browser you want to stick with, then it's a good idea to make it your default browser on your computer or mobile device. How to do that is beyond the scope of this book and varies between operating systems, so you might want to get some help with the process. The reason you want to do this is because if you click on a link within an email, for example, your computer will use its default web browser to open the website, so you want to make sure it's using the right browser. Another option is to uninstall the browsers you don't want so you only have one. Keep in mind that many operating systems won't let you uninstall their built-in browser.

**Search Engines**

Now that you have an idea of what a web browser is, I will now go over search engines. A search engine is a service that allows you to search for content on the Internet via a web browser. There are many companies that provide this service free of charge for you to use. The search engine providers "crawl" the web and index its content in their own databases so when you search for a specific word or phrase, it can find the websites that match what you are looking for.

You have most likely heard of Google, and they have the most popular search engine in use today. Providing search engines is not the only thing Google does, of course, but that is how they got their start and is one of the reasons they are such a huge company today. Here is a listing of some of the more popular search engines, and there are many more out there besides the ones in my list:

- Google
- Bing (by Microsoft)
- Yahoo
- Ask
- AOL
- DuckDuckGo

To get to a search engine all you need to do is type its address\URL (discussed later in the chapter) into the address bar of your browser. Or you can even use one search engine to do a search for a different search engine. For example, in figure 2.2 I used the Google search engine to do a search for Bing (the results are shown in figure 2.3). (I will get into more details about how to do web searches in Chapter 3.)

Figure 2.2

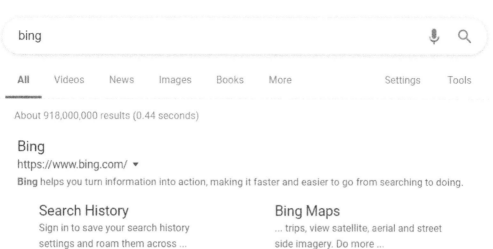

Figure 2.3

Then when I click on the first result for Bing it will take me to www.bing.com, where I will then see something similar to figure 2.4. Then I can type in my search criteria in their search box and do my searches from there.

Figure 2.4

 When trying out different search engines, you will notice that some like to have other content on the page such as news stories or pictures, while others (like Google) get right to the point and just have a search box.

Using different search engines will yield different results for your searches since they are not all sharing the same information and build their databases and crawl the Internet differently from each other. So, if you are not getting the results you are looking for from one particular search engine, then you might want to try another. (I will go over how to perform effective searches in Chapter 3.)

**Tabbed Browsing**

One of the greatest inventions when it comes to web browsers is the addition of tabs which let you have more than one website open at a time. In the old days, if you wanted to be on two or more websites at a time, you would have to open multiple instances of your web browser. For those of us who have multiple websites open all day long, that can get messy, but thanks to tabbed browsing, things are a lot more organized and easier.

Figure 2.5 shows the Google Chrome web browser open with a single default tab. You will always have at least one tab open when using any web browser. Since my home page is set to google.com when I open my browser, it automatically goes to their website.

Figure 2.5

Next to that tab is a **+** sign, which is what I would click on to open up a new tab within my browser. Doing this does not close the existing tab, but rather opens up an additional one next to it (as seen in figure 2.6). Now I have Google open in the first tab, and www.onlinecomputertips.com open in the second tab, and I can go back and forth between them. By the way, most browsers will open your default home page when you click on a new tab.

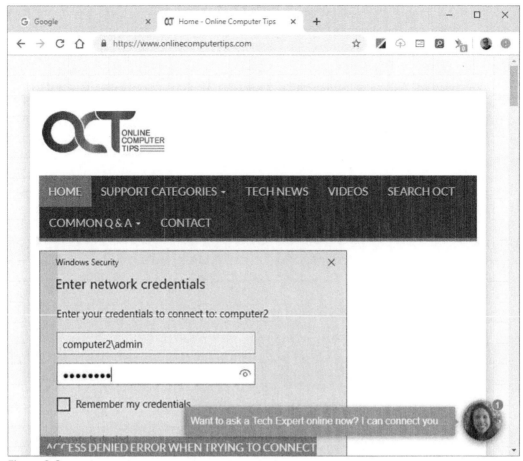

Figure 2.6

As you can see in figure 2.7, you can have as many tabs open as you want and switch back and forth between them. So, if you like to have your email, news, Facebook, YouTube, etc. pages all open at the same time, it's very easy to do.

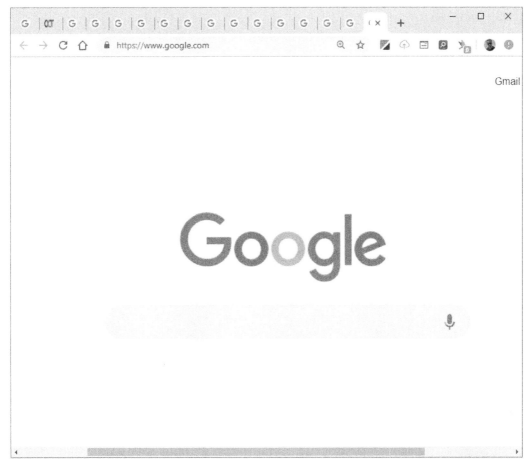

Figure 2.7

If you don't like the order that your tabs are open in, most browsers will let you drag them around to rearrange them however you see fit. And if you want to close a particular tab, simply click on the X on the tab itself and it will leave the others open. If you want to close all of them, then you can either do so one by one, or simply close your web browser altogether.

Many web browsers will allow you to configure them to remember what tabs you had open the next time you launch the browser. So, if you like to have the same ten tabs open every time you start your computer or re-open your web browser, then that is something you can do fairly easily.

**Bookmarks\Favorites**

Most, if not all, Internet users will have websites that they like to go to on a regular basis. But rather than have to remember what they are or what the website name is, they use bookmarks (or favorites as they are sometimes called) to save these websites in their web browser for easy access. Once you create a bookmark all you need to do is click on it and it will take you to the exact website and section of that website that you were on when you created it.

These bookmarks are created and accessed differently depending on what web browser you are using, but the process is very similar between all of them. For example, figure 2.8 shows how to add the current page to your bookmarks by clicking on the three vertical dots at the top right of the browser window, and then choosing *Bookmarks* and the *Bookmark this page* option. You can also use the Ctrl-D keyboard shortcut as it shows on the very right of the menu item.

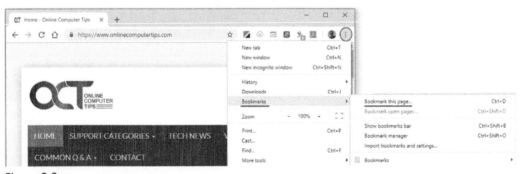

Figure 2.8

When you add a bookmark, you are prompted to give it a name or keep the name that it chooses, which is based off the webpage you are bookmarking. If you have bookmark folders, you can choose to have the bookmark be placed in a specific folder.

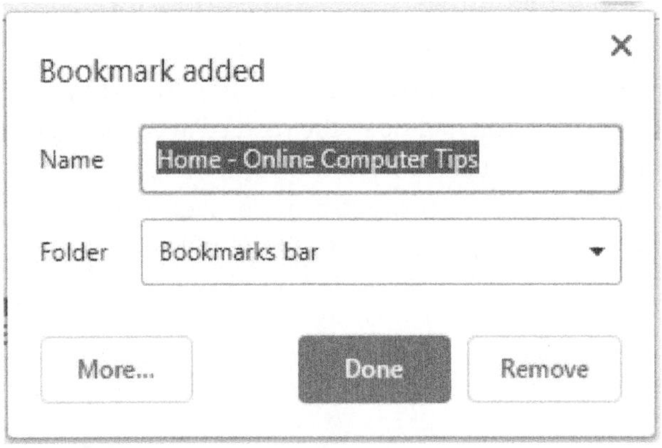

Figure 2.9

Figure 2.10 shows you how to add a favorite in Microsoft Edge by clicking the star icon to the right of the website's address. Remember that bookmarks and favorites are the same thing, and Microsoft is the one who usually refers to them as "favorites" while most other browsers use the term "bookmarks".

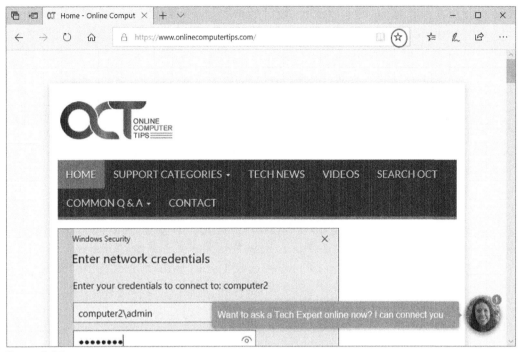

Figure 2.10

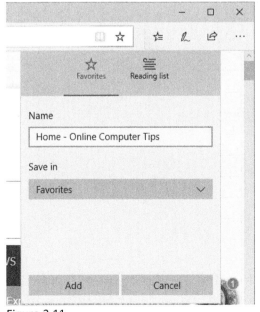

Figure 2.11

Most web browsers will also let you have a bookmark toolbar at the top of the browser where you can have your most commonly used bookmarks listed so you can simply click on the one you want without having to take the extra steps to go to your bookmark menu.

It is possible and fairly easy to import your bookmarks from one browser to a different browser by exporting them from one and importing them from another. That way you have the same bookmarks on multiple browsers, but keep in mind that if you add a new one to one browser, it won't add it to any others automatically. Some browsers (like Google Chrome) will apply your bookmarks to any copy of Chrome you open from different devices as long as you are logged into your Google account. This way you just need to have your bookmarks on your desktop, for example, and when you open Chrome on your laptop, your bookmarks will be synchronized and show up there as well.

The process to access your bookmarks will vary depending on what browser you use, but all you really need to do is find where they are kept and click on the one you want to go to. Figure 2.12 shows how to access your bookmarks (favorites) using Microsoft Edge. It's also possible to edit your bookmarks to do things like rename them, delete them, and even change the address of where they point to.

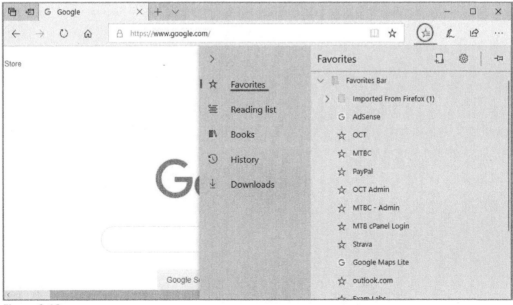

Figure 2.12

Figure 2.13 shows the bookmark manager from the Google Chrome web browser. If I click on the three vertical dots next to a bookmark name, I have options to do things such as edit, copy the URL (address), delete, and open the bookmark. Figure 2.14 shows how it looks if I choose the *Edit* option. From here I can change the bookmark name or the address of that bookmark.

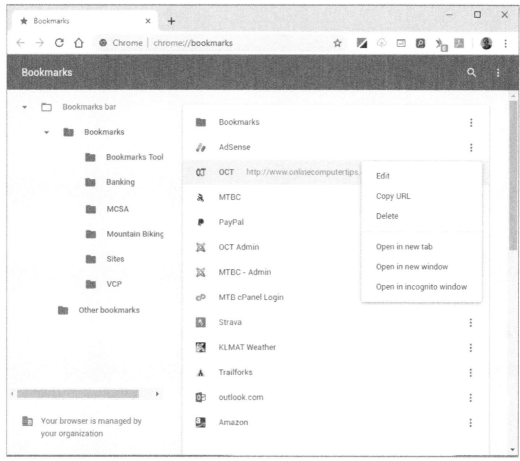

Figure 2.13

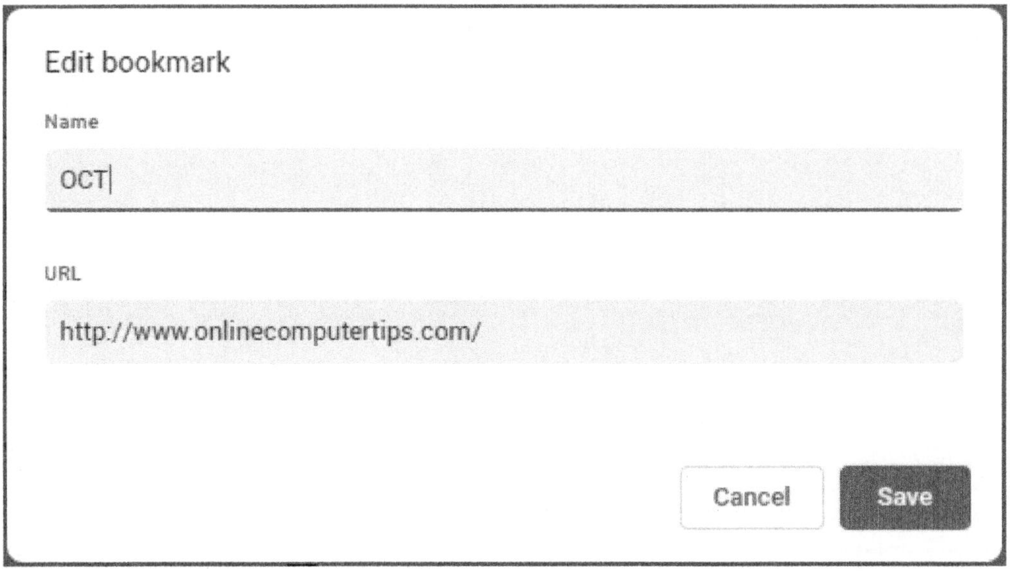

Figure 2.14

Figure 2.15 shows the options I get when clicking the three vertical dots at the very top of the Chrome browser window. Here I can do things like sort the bookmarks by name (alphabetical order) and also add a new folder to organize my bookmarks. The import and export bookmark options can also be found here.

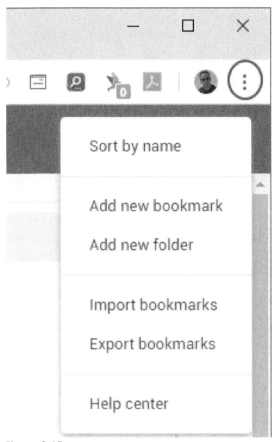

Figure 2.15

When you export your bookmarks they are usually exported as an html file, which is a web page file. Then you can import this html file into a different browser and have your bookmarks there as well.

**Website Addresses\URLs**

All websites have addresses that are friendly names we use to connect to a web server located somewhere in the world. Like I mentioned before, DNS translates these website names\addresses into the complex number (IP address) that takes you to the actual web server itself. The official name for these website addresses are URLs, which stands for *Uniform Resource Locator*.

URLs are the path to a particular page on a particular website. For example, the address **microsoft.com** will take you to the main Microsoft website, but the address **microsoft.com/operatingsystems/windows10** will take you to the Windows 10 page in the sub-category operating systems of the Microsoft website. When you click on a link on a webpage it will take you to the address associated

31

with that link so you don't need to know what it is or type it in yourself, so this is more informational than anything else.

You might have heard the term "domain name" being tossed around before, and that is the registered name used by that company on the internet. So, in this example, the domain is microsoft.com, and anything after that is a part of that domain. You will even come across situations where there is something before the domain name such as ***sales*.microsoft.com**.

 You might have noticed that some website addresses have www in front of them while others don't, but you can still get to that website. This is because the people running the site configured it so if you don't put www in front of the name, it will take you to the web server of that domain by default.

For the most part, you can just use the term "website address" rather than URL so you don't confuse anyone since they are pretty much the same thing. So if you know the address of the website you want to go to, you can type it into the address bar of the browser, press enter on your keyboard, and it will take you to that website (assuming you spelled it correctly).

Figure 2.16

You can also highlight the address in the address bar and copy and paste it into another browser, another tab, email, document, or anywhere else you can copy and paste text. (I will discuss sharing websites in Chapter 3.)

**Cookies**
Everyone loves cookies right? Unfortunately, when you hear the word "cookies" when talking about web browsers and the Internet, it's not quite as delicious.

Cookies play an important part when it comes to your Internet activity and how your browsing experience goes. Cookies are small files that are placed on your computer by websites and are used by the website as a way for it to be able to recognize you and keep track of your preferences for that site. These cookies can either be temporary for the current visit to the site, or permanent so it can be used the next time you go to that site.

These cookies can store various types of information and can be helpful, for the most part, even though there are many that can do things like track your web browsing history to be used for gathering information about you for advertising purposes, etc. For the most part, they store things like your name, email address, and other information so the next time you go to that website you don't need to enter it in again. One common thing that a cookie can do is keep track of the items you have in your cart while you are shopping online, so if you close your browser before checking out and open it again, the items will still be in your cart and you don't have to start over.

It *is* possible to delete your cookies if you don't want them storing information about you and your online habits on your computer. Some third party cleaning programs will even let you delete just the cookies you want to get rid of while keeping others that you want to keep. To remove cookies from your web browser look for the section that lets you clear your browsing history and see if there is an option for cookies as well, since not all browsers work the same way when it comes to cleanup. Figure 2.17 shows the *clear browsing data* dialog box from Google Chrome, and you can see how there is a section to remove the cookies from your computer. (I will be discussing browsing history and clearing saved data in Chapter 3.)

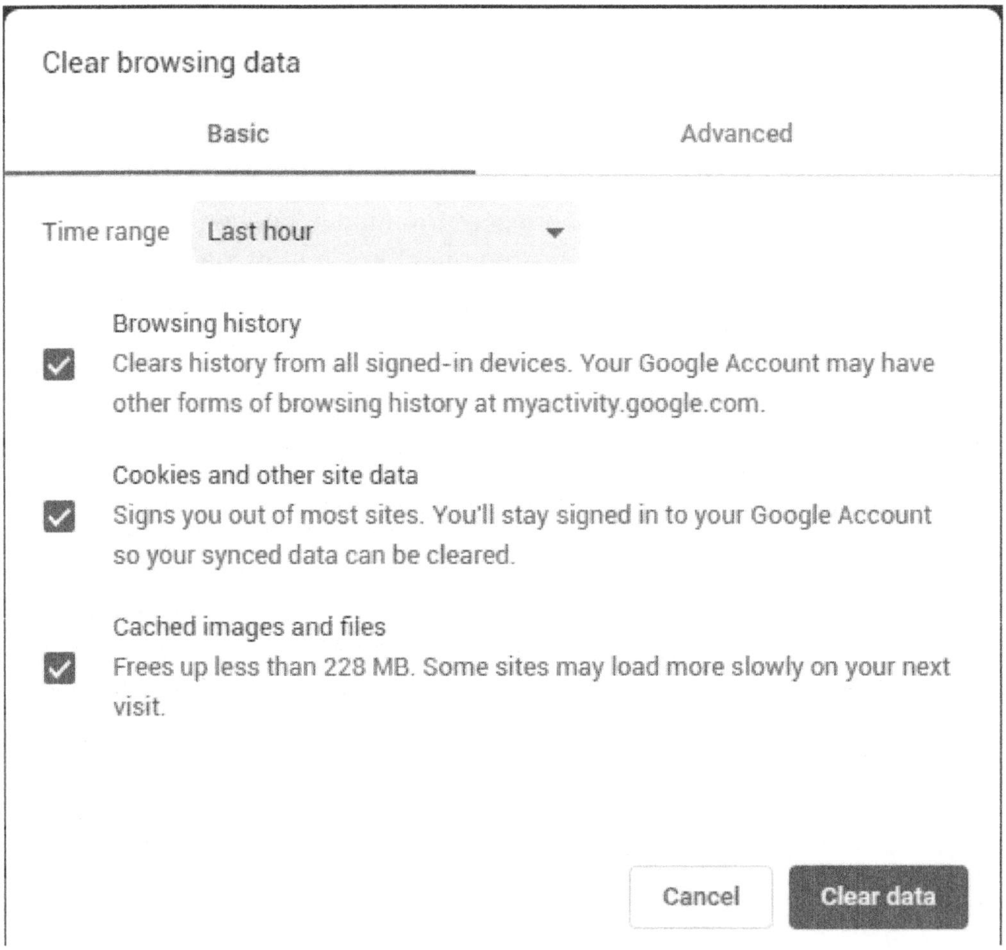

Clear browsing data

| Basic | Advanced |
| --- | --- |

Time range    Last hour ▼

☑ Browsing history
Clears history from all signed-in devices. Your Google Account may have
other forms of browsing history at myactivity.google.com.

☑ Cookies and other site data
Signs you out of most sites. You'll stay signed in to your Google Account
so your synced data can be cleared.

☑ Cached images and files
Frees up less than 228 MB. Some sites may load more slowly on your next
visit.

Cancel       Clear data

Figure 2.17

**Storing Form Information and Passwords**
The last thing I want to go over in this chapter is how you can save form
information and passwords within your browser to make things easier and more
convenient for you. But doing so may come at a cost!

Most, if not all, web browsers will let you store things such as addresses,
passwords, and payment methods within the browser so you don't need to do
things like type in your address on an order form, remember your password for a
shopping site, or break out your wallet to make an online purchase. You may have
noticed when signing up for an online account of some sort where you create a
username and password that your browser might have asked you if you would like
it to remember the new login information you created. If you say *yes*, then the
next time you go to that website's login page the username and password will
automatically be filled in for you.

Another thing you might have noticed is when you go to fill in an online form with your name and address that your browser will offer to complete it for you with the information it has stored from a previous form you have filled out. This can come in very handy if you are the type who doesn't like to type!

One downside to this convenience is the potential security risk involved. I will have an entire chapter on safety and security coming up, but for now I just wanted to mention that it's not a good idea to store login information and form information for certain sites in case your computer gets compromised.

Fortunately, if you have some stored information that you want to clear out, then you should be able to remove it from your web browser without too much effort. For example, figure 2.18 shows the Autofill settings for Google Chrome, and you can go into each one and see what passwords, payment methods, and addresses it has stored for you and remove the ones you don't want. You can also disable the ability for your browser to remember this type of information.

Figure 2.18

# Chapter 3 – Surfing the Internet

Now that you have a better understating of the more technical side of web browsers and search engines, it's time to start seeing what kind of cool stuff we can find out on the Internet. Speaking of cool, the phrase "surfing the Internet" is kind of outdated, so if you want to look cool in front of others, you might want to avoid using it. (I still like it though!)

**How to Perform Effective Searches**
There is more to searching the Internet than just putting in a word or phrase and pressing enter to see your results. Sure it will work fine for the most part, but there are other methods you can use to get more accurate results. On the other hand, if you can find what you need with simple searches then that's ok too, since most of the time that is what I do as well.

When typing in a word or phrase into a search engine, it will search for all of those words no matter what order you type them in. So if you type in **top rated dog food**, your results will be the same as if you typed in **dog rated food top,** as you can see in figures 3.1 and 3.2.

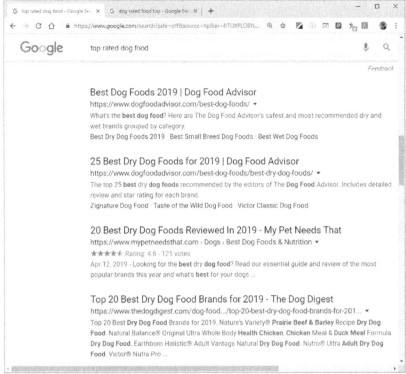

Figure 3.1

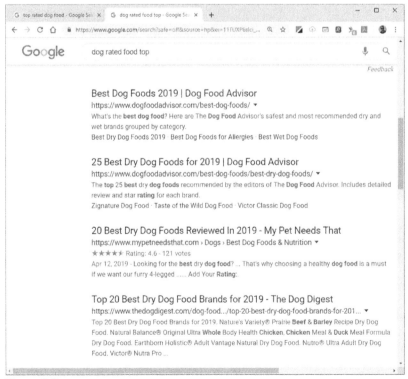

Figure 3.2

You want to be as specific as you can to avoid getting irrelevant results or too many results that you will have to sift through to find what you need. Many times you can even do your search in the form of a question, such as *what is the best computer for gaming* or *how do I make chicken alfredo* because it might be a commonly asked question or search term.

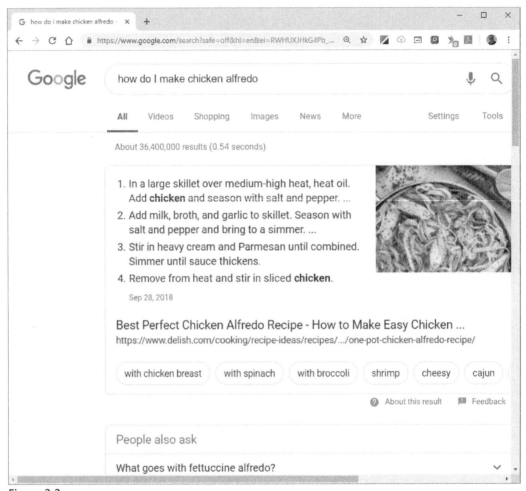

Figure 3.3

There are many tricks you can use to improve your search results, and I will now go over some of the more useful ones which you can then try out and see how they work for you.

*Stay away from common words*
Google ignores most common words and characters such as "and" and "to", as well as certain single letters and digits because they tend to slow down your

search without improving the search results. So try and design your searches to use more unique words that will give you less generic and unrelated results.

*Use quotation marks for phrases*

If you put quotes around your search phrase, then Google will find results that contain all of the words in the exact order you have entered them in the search box. For example, if you wanted to look up pages on Bill Gates but didn't want to get results containing other people named Bill or results about gates, you could type in "Bill Gates" and Google will find pages with that exact phrase in it. You do not need to worry about capitalization either. You can also use this for longer phrases such as "blue 1969 Camaro z28" if you wanted to get specific. Notice in figure 3.4 how Google found images matching blue 1969 Camaro z28, and also the exact phrase, which it highlighted in bold within the search results.

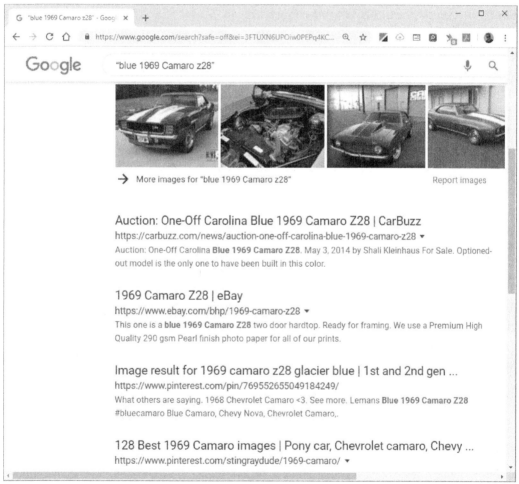

Figure 3.4

*Using the "+" search variable*

If you are looking for a certain thing on the Internet but need to include a specific word in your search results, then you can use the plus sign to have your browser include your keyword in its results. For example, if you were looking up mountain bikes and wanted to include Trek brand bikes in your search, you can type in **mountain bikes + trek** in the search box. Just make sure you put a space before the +.

*Using **OR** to find two results*

To find pages that include either of two search terms, add an uppercase **OR** between the terms. For example, if you wanted information about Princeton or Harvard University, you can search by **university Princeton OR Harvard**. Just make sure you use an uppercase OR.

*Searching all the pages of an entire website*

If you wanted to bring up a listing of every page for a certain site, you can use the **site:** search string. An example would be **site:www.onlinecomputertips.com**, which would list every page on the onlinecomputertips.com site that was indexed by the search engine. Keep in mind that this may give you more than you need depending on how many pages are indexed.

*Domain search*

You can also use the **site:** query to search for a specific item within only one specific website by entering the search terms you're looking for, followed by the word "site" and a colon followed by the domain name. For example, here is how you'd find information about Mustangs on the Ford website. Type in **mustang site:www.ford.com.**

*Searching by title*

To find all pages with a certain word or phrase in the title of the page, you can use the **intitle:** query. For example, if you were to type in **intitle:australian shepherds**, that would show results for pages with Australian shepherds in the title of the search results.

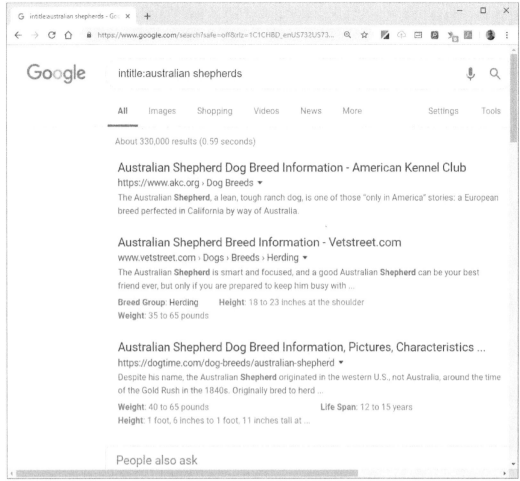

Figure 3.5

Of course there are many more tricks of the trade you can use to narrow down your searches, but these should be enough to get you the results you are looking for, so give them a try and see how they work for you.


**Deciphering Search Results**
Searching the Internet is one thing, but trying to figure out what the results of your searches mean is a whole other issue. For the most part, search engines do a pretty good job of getting you the most accurate results based on your search terms, but they can still be a little confusing. Plus, with the abundance of advertisements being placed everywhere online, you will need to know the difference between a useful result and something that is just trying to get your money.

The results you get will vary depending on what search engine you are using. You may or may not also be presented with other results from your search related to things like shopping or images. For example, figure 3.6 shows a Google search result for the phrase **tan area rug** with its 57,100,000 results.

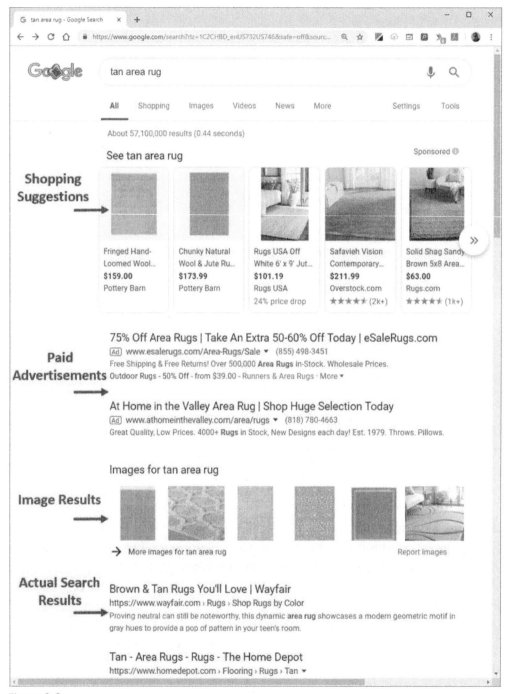

Figure 3.6

The first part of the results show shopping options that you can click on to find places where you can buy rugs. The next section consists of paid advertisements that other companies pay Google to display when people search for things that apply to them. You can tell these are advertisements because they have the word Ad next to the address. These may or may not be what you are looking for, and just because they come up at the top of the search results doesn't mean they are the best choice to click on.

Next, you will get image results that match your search in case you were wanting to see images related to tan area rugs. (This would be more useful if you were doing a search for something a little more exciting like beach vacation spots.) Finally, you get the actual search results where you can start looking for the websites that will give you the information you are looking for.

At the bottom of the page (figure 3.7) you might see things like local businesses that sell rugs if you are logged into your Google account and it knows your location. You may also see more ads at the bottom as well. At the *very* bottom you will get some suggestions for related searches that you might want to use to improve your search results. You can click on any of them to do a search for that phrase.

If you take a look at the bottom of figure 3.7 you will see that there are many pages of search results that you can go through to find what you are looking for. Many people tend to only look at the first page or two because as you get into some of the later pages the results tend to not apply as well, but that doesn't mean they aren't worth checking out.

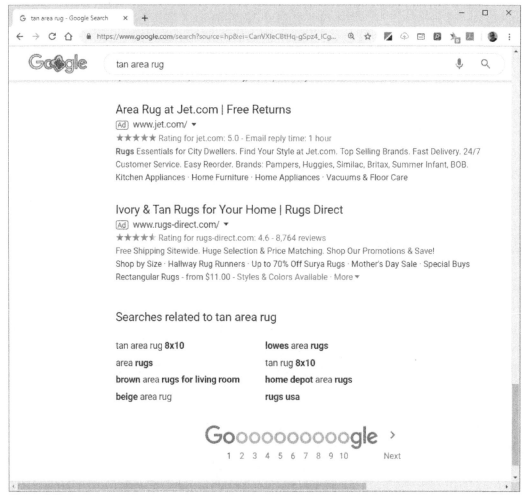

Figure 3.7

Now I will perform the same search using the Yahoo search engine to see what their results look like. To do so, I will need to go to the Yahoo website, which is yahoo.com, or I can just do a search from Google for Yahoo. Figure 3.8 shows the results of the search, but notice how the layout differs from what Google gave me. You still get similar items such as paid advertisements and shopping suggestions, but they are laid out differently.

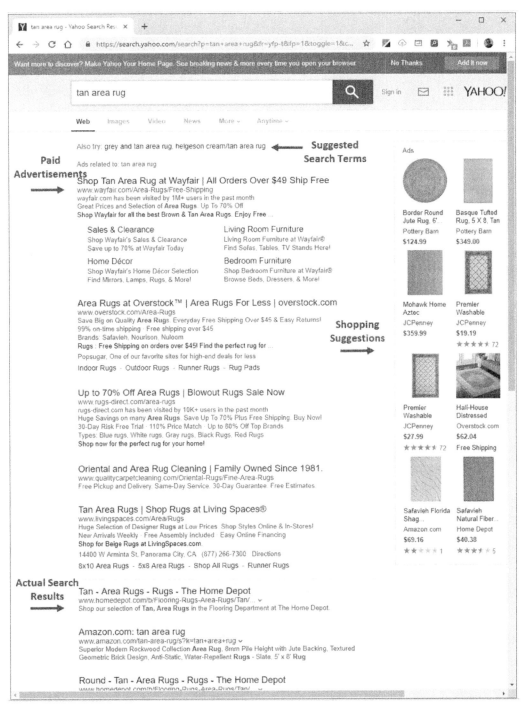

Figure 3.8

 If you take a look at the top of figure 3.8 you will see that Yahoo is asking if I want it to be my default search engine (I use Google for that). If I were to say yes, then it would change the home page of my web browser to the Yahoo website, so be careful when presented with these types of questions.

Figure 3.9 shows the bottom of the page for the Yahoo search results. Once again, there are more paid advertisements, suggested search terms, and additional page numbers. Notice how there are only 9,300,000 results compared to the 57,100,000 results from Google.

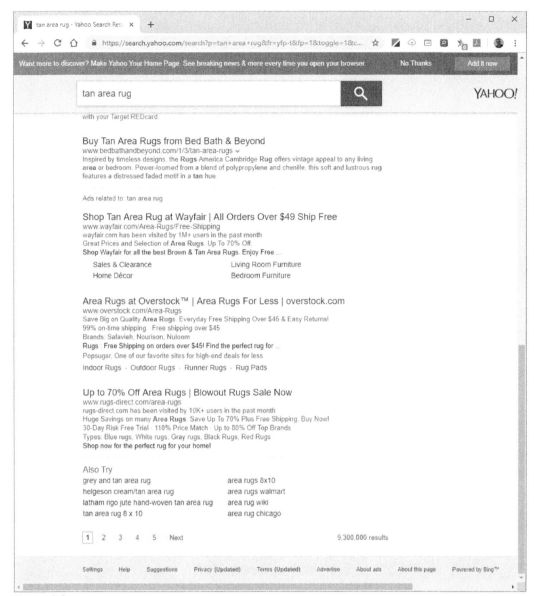

Figure 3.9

As you can see, you will get varying results for your searches based on what search engine you use, so you might want to try out a few to see which one you like the best. It doesn't matter what web browser you are using, and you will get the same results if you are doing your searches on Google using Edge, Firefox, Safari, etc.

Now I would like to talk about the other categories that you can click on for your search term that most search engines offer. Figure 3.10 shows a search for **sailboat** in Google, but take a look at the categories below the search box. You can click on any one of them to search within that category.

47

Figure 3.10

For example, if I click on **Images**, I get the results show below. Notice how there are other ways to fine-tune the image search above the results such as only displaying clipart or wooden sailboats.

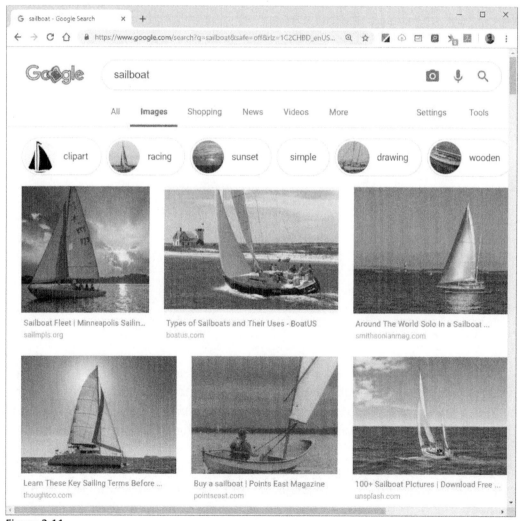

Figure 3.11

Next, I will click on **Shopping**, and here is what I get.

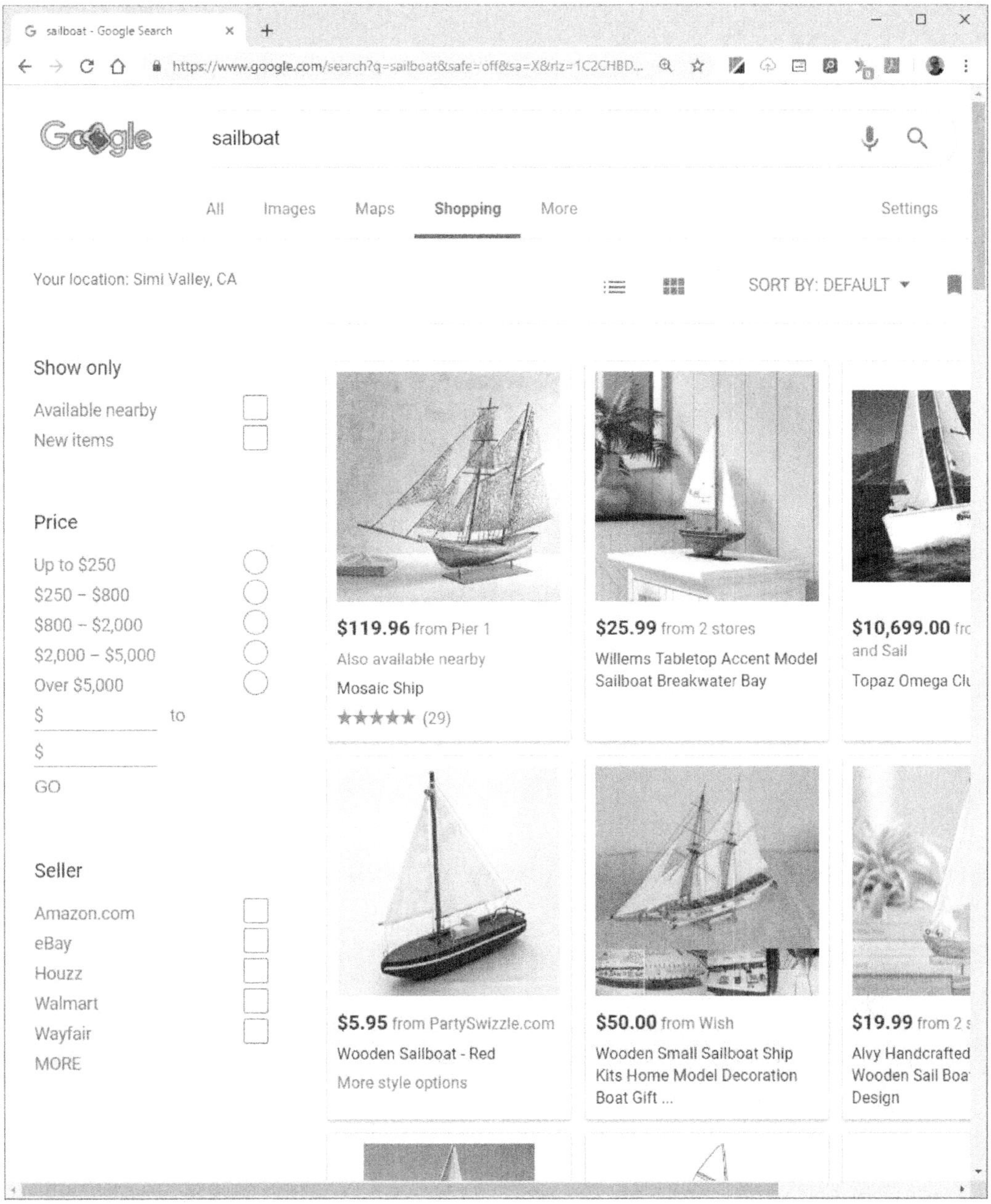

Figure 3.12

Now I will click on **Videos** to see what types of videos there are out there related to sailboats.

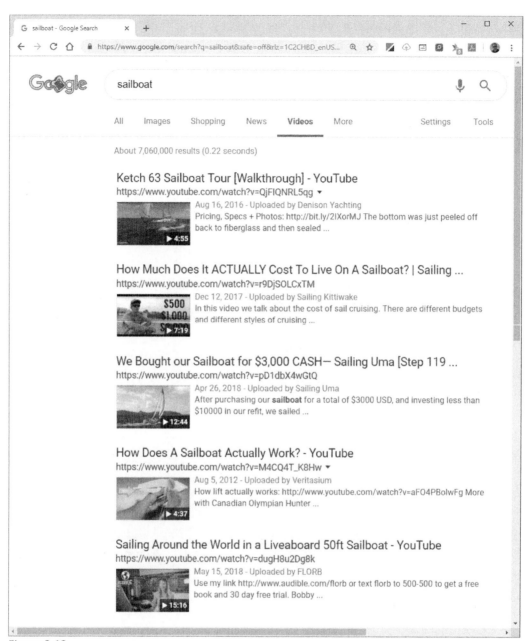

Figure 3.13

Then there are other categories you can choose from, and they can vary depending on what search engine you are using, as you can see from the images below.

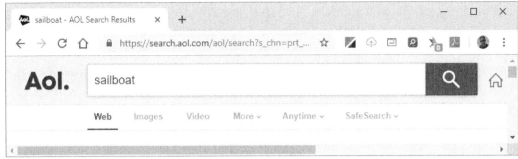
Figure 3.14

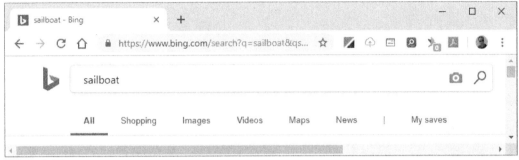
Figure 3.15

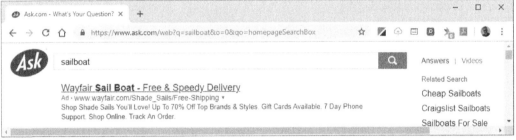
Figure 3.16

So, as you can see, it's fairly easy to get different types of information from your search, so you can find pretty much anything you are looking for.

## Saving Pictures and Text From Websites

When searching for things on the Internet, you might feel the need to want to save a particular image or paragraph of text to use later. This is a very easy process to do, but just like with everything else, the process can vary depending on what web browser you are using and if you are on a Windows PC, Mac, or mobile device.

If you are doing a specific image search, then I suggest that you use the images feature of whatever search engine you are using for the best results. Once you find the image, you want to make sure that you are saving the best quality version and not just a smaller thumbnail version. For example, if you look at figure 3.17, you will see a bunch of Australian Shepherd dog images, and let's say you want to save the first one. If you did save it, then it would be a lower quality\smaller image than you would get if you clicked on it to have it show full size (like in figure 3.18).

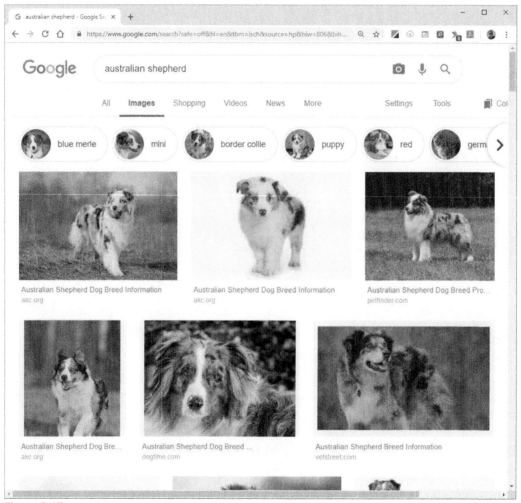

Figure 3.17

Notice how it says 729 x 468 below the image? That is the size of the image in pixels, and the larger the numbers, the bigger the image will be, and most likely the better the quality.

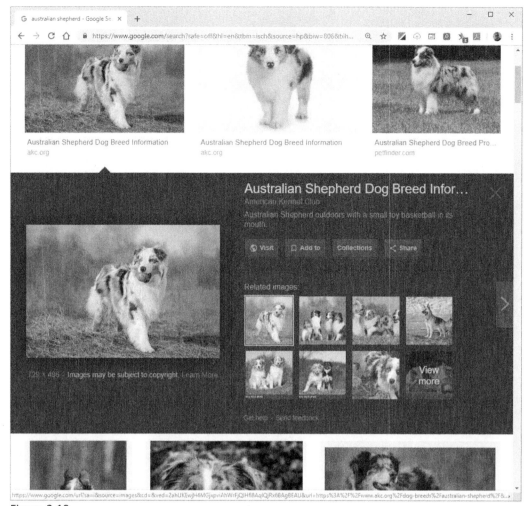

Figure 3.18

If you want to see the image full size, you can right click on it and choose *Open image in new tab*, and it will show the image by itself at its real size. Like I mentioned earlier, your results will vary based on what web browser you are using and what search engine. For my examples I am using Google's search engine with the Google Chrome browser.

Figure 3.19

Now that I have the image full size, it's time to save it to the hard drive on my computer so I can use it later. To do so, right click anywhere on the picture and choose *Save image as* (or save pictures as) and select a location on your computer that you will remember and be able to find later. You can also stick with the default file name, or type in anything you wish. Many people just save images to their desktop or pictures folder.

Figure 3.20

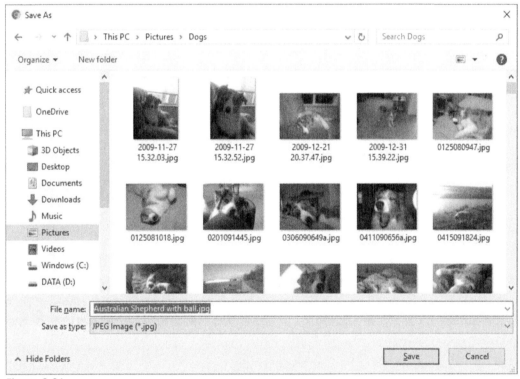

Figure 3.21

If you ever find an image that doesn't have any save options when you right click on it, that is most likely because they have disabled the saving feature for that web page. Not everyone wants to share their pictures, and it's not always legal to use other people's images for your own work.

There are ways to fine-tune your image search for better results, and some search engines will have these features while others won't. For example, in Google Chrome you can click on the Tools button to get more options to help you customize your results. For example, you can search for a specific image size, so if you only want high quality pictures you can choose *large*. Or if you want to find only clipart, you can change the *Type* to clipart.

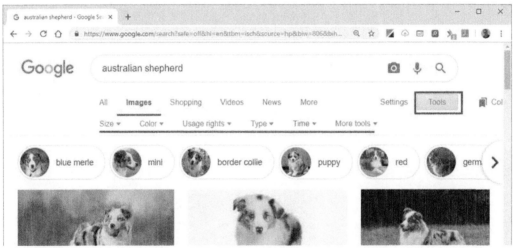

Figure 3.22

Another cool feature that Chrome offers is the right click *Search Google for image* option. This can be used to do a Google search for other versions or copies of that same image in case you would like to see if you can find a better version of the picture.

Figure 3.23

Figure 3.24 shows the results of the Google image search. As you can see, it found other sizes of the image, and you can click on the size you want to show the results. It also found images that are similar to the one I was searching for as well as websites that contain that specific image.

Figure 3.24

When it comes to saving text from a website, it is a much simpler process, and if you can copy and paste text from a document or email, then you shouldn't have any problem with this procedure.

Let's say I am on a particular website and found some useful information that I want to include in a document I am creating on mountain bike trails. I have found the website I want to get the information from and have located the text that I want to save. So all I need to do is use my mouse to highlight the text (as shown in figure 3.25), then right click anywhere on the highlighted text and choose Copy. (I can also use the *Ctrl-C* keyboard shortcut for Windows users, or *Command-C* for Mac users.)

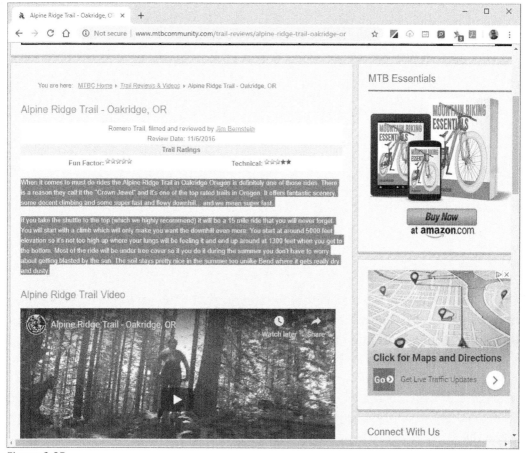

Figure 3.25

Now I want to save the text I copied into a Microsoft Word document, so I go over to my Word document and paste it in. I can either right click where I want the text to go and choose Paste, or I can use the *Ctrl-V* shortcut for Windows or *Command-V* shortcut for Mac.

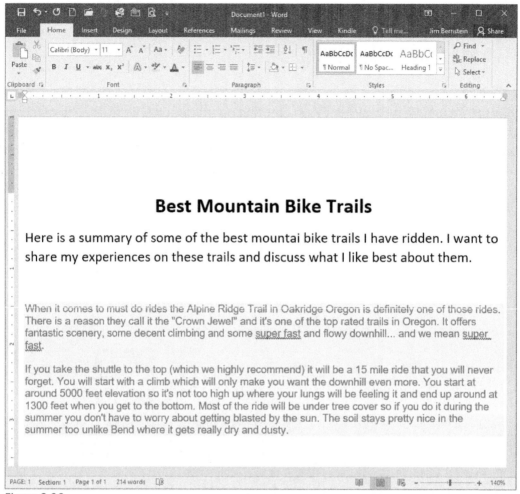

Figure 3.26

One issue you might run into is that when you paste the text into wherever you may want to place it, it will most likely keep the text formatting of the web page and not match up with the rest of your document (as you can see in figure 3.26). If this happens, then you will have to highlight the text that you just pasted in and change the font and formatting to match your other text. Or you can use the *paste as plain text* option from the program you are pasting the text into. How you do that will depend on the program, but many times you will have that option when using the *right click>Paste* option.

## Right Click Options

I have been discussing how to save images and text by right clicking with your mouse, but there are other right click options you can use within your web browser that I want to discuss that you might find helpful as well. Once again, the options you will get will depend on the web browser you are using!

Going back to the discussion on copying text from a website, if you right click on the highlighted text, you will get additional options. Here is what you will typically see in different web browsers:

### Google Chrome

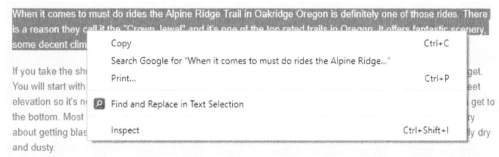

Figure 3.27

### Microsoft Edge

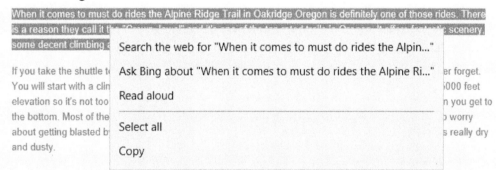

Figure 3.28

### Mozilla Firefox

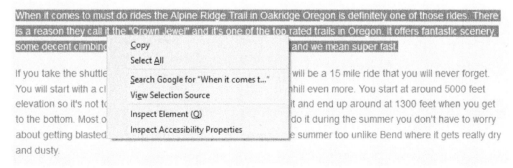

Figure 3.29

As you can see, the options are a bit different between the web browsers, and some of the choices such as *Inspect* and *View Selection Source* you will never use. Also keep in mind that if you are browsing on a mobile device, you won't have any way to right click, so this doesn't really apply. As for right clicking on images, you will get different options between browsers as well, so feel free to try them out and see what options you have.

You can also use the right click method to find additional options for links in your search result, or even links on other web pages themselves. Figure 3.30 shows the options when right clicking on a link in Google Chrome.

As you can see, you can choose the *Open link in new tab option*, which will open a new tab within Chrome and load the page that is associated with that link. Or you can have Chrome open that page in an entirely new window, which means it will open up another copy of Chrome and load that page. *Open link in incognito window* will open that link in a private browsing window, which I will discuss in Chapter 9.

*Save link as* will save an actual copy of the page associated with that link, and you will most likely never use this option. *Copy link address* is handy if you want to send the link to someone via email, etc. (I will be getting into more detail on this later in the chapter.)

Figure 3.30

Figure 3.31 shows the right click link options for Microsoft Edge. As you can see the options are similar but not exactly the same. For example, Edge offers you the opportunity to use the Bing search engine to find out more information about the subject since Bing is owned by Microsoft as well.

Figure 3.31

Figure 3.32 shows the right click options in Firefox, which are different from Chrome and Edge. If you used other browsers, you would most likely get different options along with many of the same options.

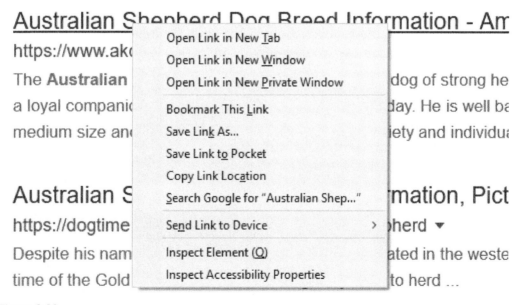

Figure 3.32

**Finding Directions**

One of the best things about the Internet is the ability to find the things you need quickly, and directions are at the top of the list (at least for me!). Back in the old days, if you wanted to get somewhere, you would either need to call for directions and write them down on a piece of paper, or break out the old map and try and figure it out. Now it's as simple as putting in the destination address of where you want to go and hitting the road.

If you have used the GPS on your phone for directions, then you should already be familiar with this process. One difference between your phone and your computer is that your phone knows where you are, but your computer most likely doesn't. Some services (like Google, for example) will let you set a home location in your profile so that when you are logged into your Google account in your browser, it will use it to find things around you that you are searching for. For example, if you do a search for steak houses, it will find the ones in your area and display them in your search results and also on a map. Then you can click on the one you want to get more information about it and also get directions right to it.

Once again, I will be using the Google search engine and the Chrome web browser to demonstrate how to find directions to a specific location. In this example I want to find out how to get to the Space Needle in Seattle. To begin, I will open up Chrome, click on the apps section at the top right, and then on Maps (figure 3.33). You can also type in maps in your search box from whatever search engine you like to use, and you can use whatever map service you like such as Bing Maps or Yahoo Maps etc.

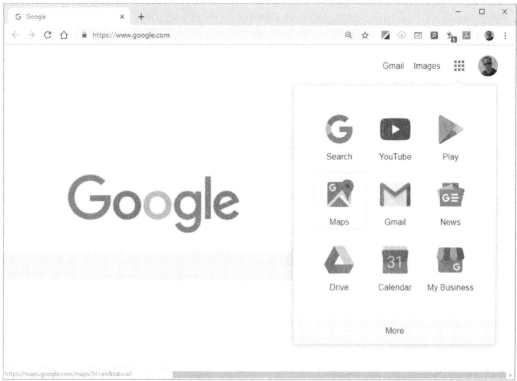

Figure 3.33

Once you open Google Maps, it will take you to your current location (if it knows where you are). You will also have the opportunity to set a home and work address if you like. The home address is used when getting directions to tell you how long it will take from home because it assumes that is where you will be starting from. The work address is used to tell you how long it will take to get to work depending on traffic conditions. You can also click on the buttons for restaurants and hotels etc. as seen in figure 3.34 to find those types of places near where you are searching.

65

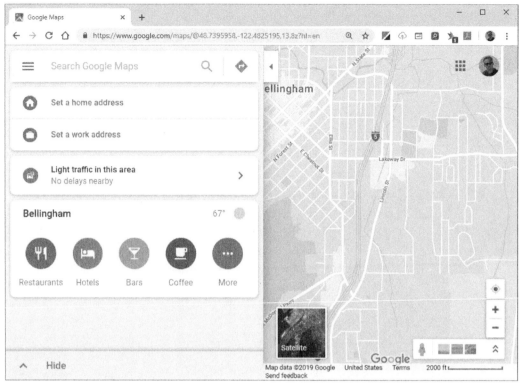

Figure 3.34

Now I will begin my quest to the Space Needle by typing in *Space Needle* in the search box. This will work because Google knows about the Space Needle, and if there were more than one, it would give me a list to choose from. It won't give you results for things like *Frank's house* because it doesn't know who you are talking about. In that case, you would need to type in Frank's address.

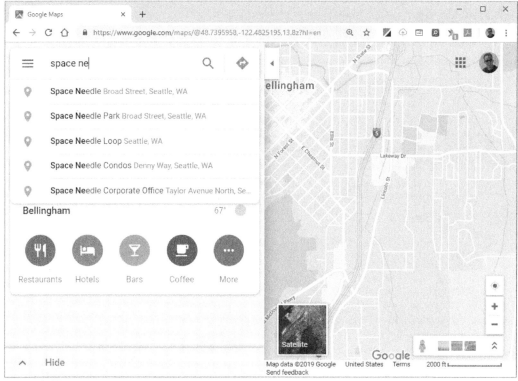

Figure 3.35

As I type in *Space Needle* it starts giving me suggestions, and I can simply click on the one I want if it appears in the list rather than type in the rest of the name. I will click on the first result since I know that is the one I am looking for.

Figure 3.36 shows what I got after choosing my destination. It shows the location on the map marked by a red marker, and also shows me points of interest around the Space Needle. You can scroll around the map and zoom in and out as needed with your mouse wheel (or pinch to zoom on your mobile device).

Take a look at all the options you get at the bottom left of the window. You can do things like get directions, save, see what's nearby, have the directions sent to your phone, and also share the location with other people. I really like the *Send to your phone* option because if you are logged in with your Google account, you can have the location sent right to your phone and then start your navigation immediately without having to search for the location on your phone.

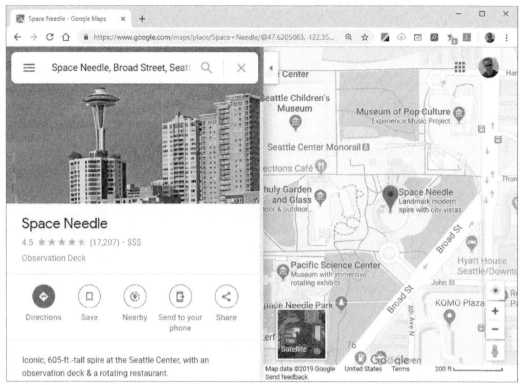

Figure 3.36

When I click on *Directions* I am prompted to enter the starting point, or in other words where I will be leaving from. I am going to enter Whidbey Island so you can see what happens if there are multiple ways to get to a specific location. Figure 3.37 shows me that there are two ways to get there. One involves taking the 5 freeway, while the other one involves taking the 405 freeway. It will highlight the fastest route, but still tell you the time and distance for each route to get there. The time it takes to get there will be based on the current traffic at the time of your search, so if you are planning on going later on in the day, it probably won't be accurate.

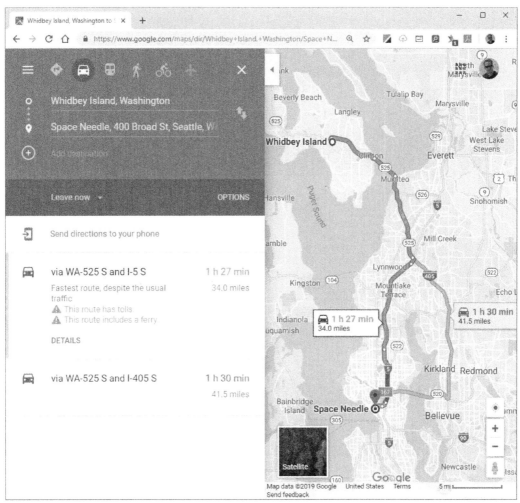

Figure 3.37

By default, Maps will assume you are driving, but if you look at the top of figure 3.37, you will see there are other options such as bus routes, riding a bike, or even walking. Figure 3.38 shows what happens if I click on bus.

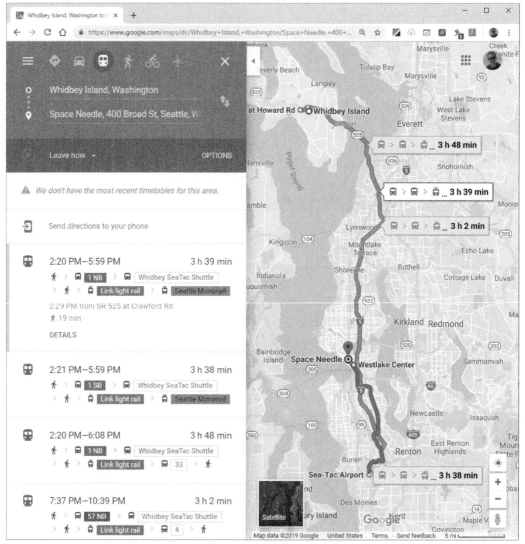

Figure 3.38

As you can see, the results change dramatically, and you now have bus schedules and the time it will take for each bus to make the trip.

Now I would like to discuss the different views you can use within Maps. I will first go to the town of Bellingham, WA and show you what Maps initially shows me (figure 3.39). It will tell you information such as the current weather, provide some photos, and also some quick facts about the area.

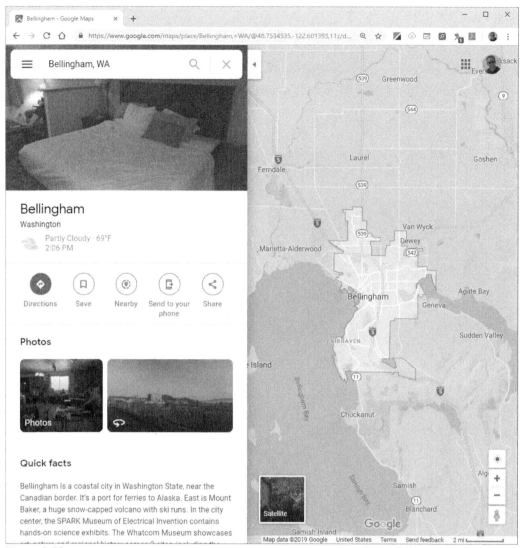

Figure 3.39

If I click on the three horizontal lines at the top of the page, it will give me many more options as to what I can do within the map (figure 3.40).

Figure 3.40

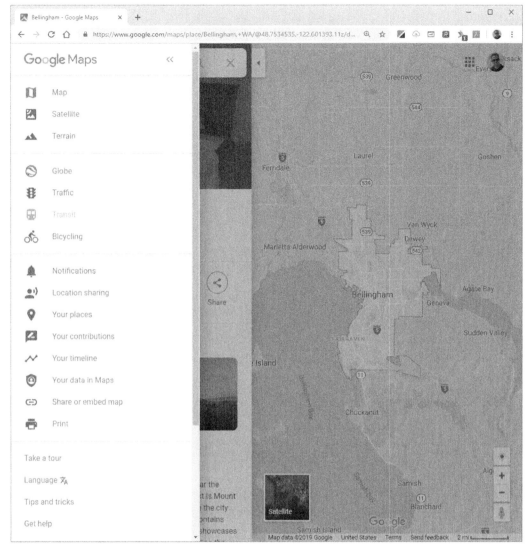

Figure 3.41

I won't go through each of these items since you may not even use Google maps but rather a different map searching service. Plus you can go through them on your own because that is a great way to learn what each item does.

I do want to show you the traffic feature since this comes in very handy when planning your trips. If you turn on the traffic layer, it will show you the current traffic on the part of the map where you are currently looking. Once again, this is the current traffic, and it most likely won't be the same later, so always have a look at the map right before you leave. As you can see in figure 3.42, it shows different colors for the levels of traffic. Green is for free flowing traffic, then orange is for mild traffic. Then you get to red for heavy traffic and dark red for very heavy traffic. The more you zoom into the map, the more detailed the traffic report will be.

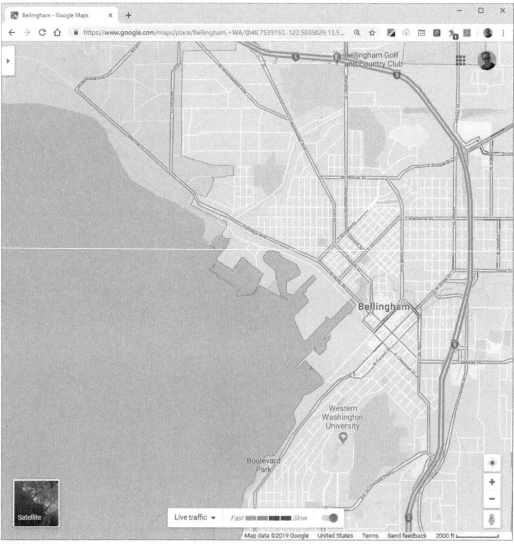

Figure 3.42

Next, I want to show you the satellite mode that Maps offers. This comes in handy if you want to see a photographic view of the area on the map so you can see landmarks that might not show up on the default map view. Plus you can see the actual buildings and roads using satellite view.

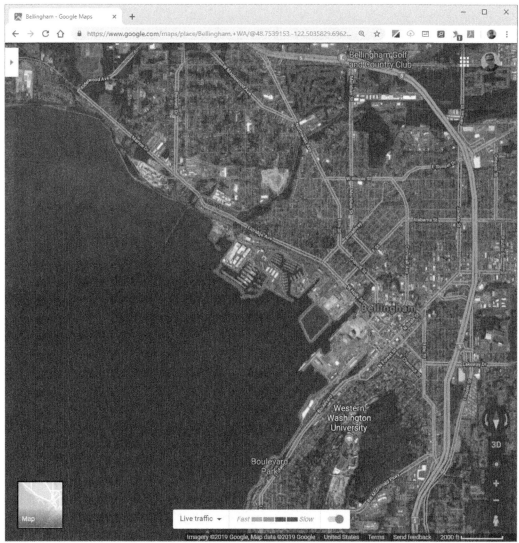

Figure 3.43

The more you zoom in, the more detailed the map becomes, and to show you this I went back to the Space Needle and zoomed in a bit (as you can see in figure 3.44).

Figure 3.44

One really cool feature of Maps is the ability to look at what they call *Street View*. Here you can see the actual view from the street outside of where you are looking at. Take a look at figure 3.44 in the lower right hand corner. You can take the little orange person figure and drag it onto a place on the street to get a street view of that location. The results are shown in figure 3.45. From there you can pan around and zoom and even go up and down the street.

Figure 3.45

You won't have the ability to do this on all streets if they have not been mapped by Google yet. You might have seen those Google maps cars driving around with the strange looking gear on the roof. These are used to map out streets to be using with their mapping service.

Figure 3.46

**Browser History**

After using your web browser of choice and going to many upon many websites, you may have the need to go back to a certain website, but might not remember what it was called. This is where browser history comes into play. Browser history is just like it sounds: a place where you can go back and see what websites you have visited in the past.

Depending on what web browser you are using, your browsing history can be kept for time periods such as 90 days, 6 months, or even longer. You can even customize how long you want your history to be kept if desired. This can be done by going to the settings and then the history section of your web browser.

How you view your history will depend on what browser you are using (of course!), but is usually pretty easy to find in all of them. For example, figure 3.47 shows the history for Google Chrome, which can be accessed by clicking on the three vertical dots at the upper right hand corner of the browser and choosing *History*. Then you will see all of your history sorted by date and time. If you want to visit a site from your history, you can simply click on the site name itself and you will be taken back to the page linked to that history item.

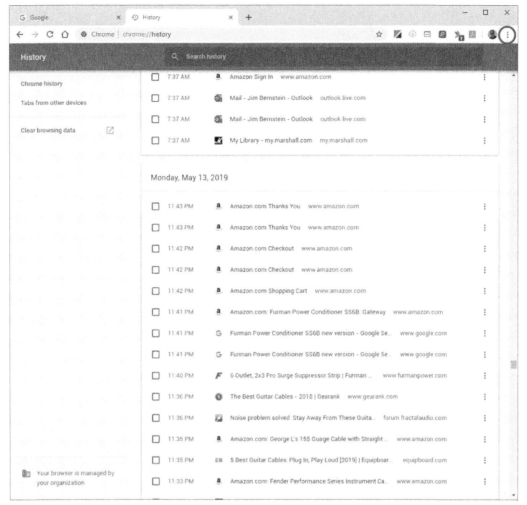

Figure 3.47

Figure 3.48 shows how you view your history in Microsoft Edge. Simply click the star icon in the toolbar and then click on the *History* section on the left. As you can see, you have the option to view history for the last hour, the current day, last week, and older by clicking the arrow next to that section. Once again, to go back to a page from your history, simply click on the history item itself.

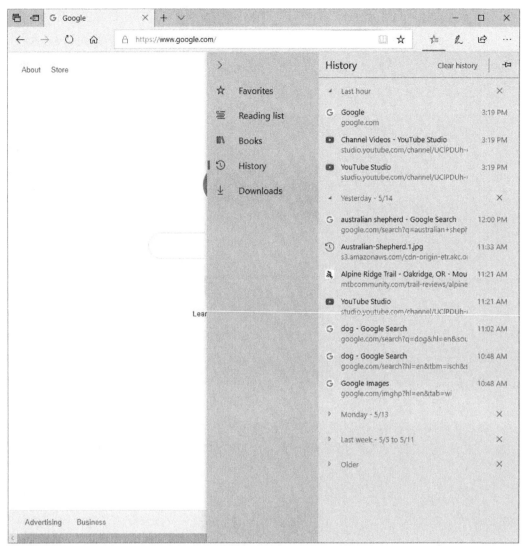

Figure 3.48

Figure 3.49 shows how the history is displayed for Mozilla Firefox when you click on the history button on the toolbar. The history is shown in order, and if you want to see more of your history, then you can click on *Show All History* at the bottom of the list and you can more options (as shown in figure 3.50).

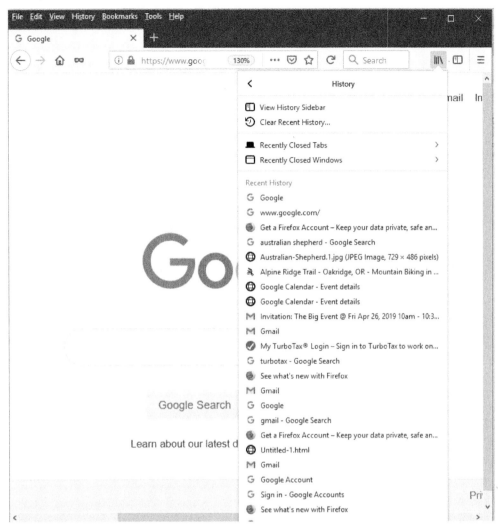

Figure 3.49

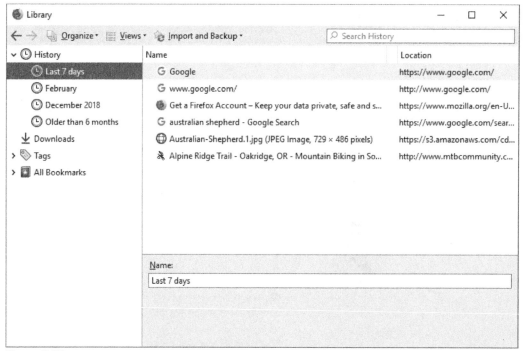

Figure 3.50

Figure 3.51 shows how the history menu looks for the Macintosh Safari web browser.

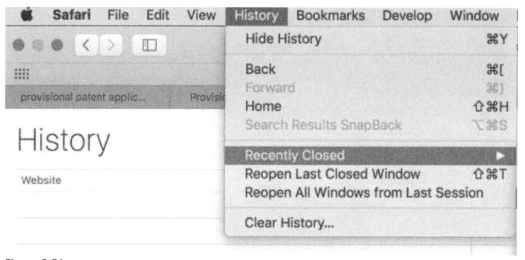

Figure 3.51

There are ways around keeping browser history if it is not something you wish to do. Plus you can easily clear your entire history, or for certain time periods or even specific entries if desired. I will go into how you do this in Chapter 9.

**Sharing Websites with Other People**

There will be many times when you are browsing the Internet and come across a website that you want to share with other people, and fortunately this is a very easy thing to do and there are a few ways to do so.

The easiest way to share a website is to copy the site's address and then paste it into something like an email or instant message chat box. If you know how to copy and paste text from something like a document, then this will be a piece of cake for you. Or if you read the section in this chapter about saving text from a website, then the same steps apply here, but the only difference will be what you are copying and pasting.

To copy a website address, what you need to do is click inside the address bar of your browser while on the page you want to share to have it highlight the address. Then you can right click anywhere on the highlighted area and choose *Copy* from the menu (as seen in figure 3.52). You can also use the shortcut keys that I went over earlier in this chapter.

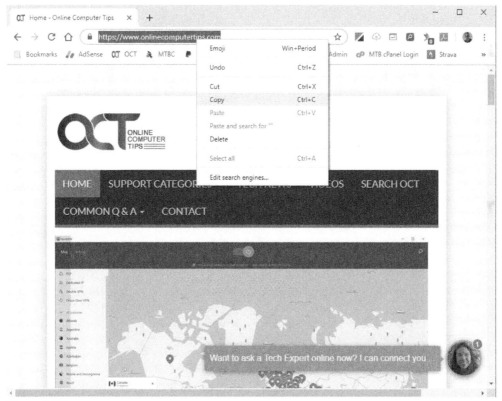

Figure 3.52

Then you will need to open up your email or the messaging program that you want to use to share the website address, paste it in there, and send it to the person or people you want to share it with. They can then click on the link from that email or message and be taken to that exact same web page.

If you are on your mobile device, then you can even share it in something like a text message. Figure 3.53 shows the menu items from Google Chrome on an Android smartphone with the *Share* option underlined. Then once I tap on *Share*, I get the options as shown in figure 3.54. As you can see, there are many ways to share the website on a mobile device.

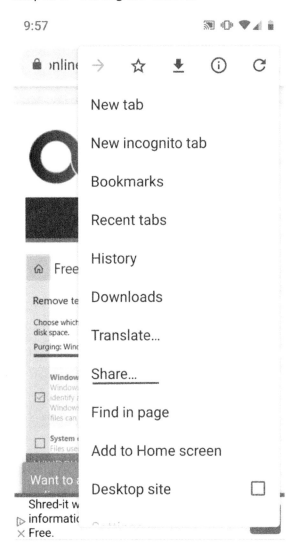

Figure 3.53

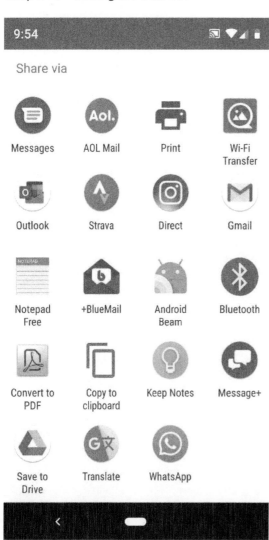

Figure 3.54

# Chapter 4 – Downloading Programs and Files

There is more to using the Internet than searching for your favorite dog pictures and checking the weather. Many people use the Internet for sharing files and downloading software to install on their computers. This topic is a little more advanced than the previous discussion, but it is something you might want to take the time to learn about because it can come in very handy.

**The Types of Files You Might Download**
There are many types of files you can download such as documents, music, videos, software updates, and so on. I'm sure at some point you have sent an email with an attachment or maybe received one with an attachment. Downloading files from the Internet is similar to saving attachments from an email, except you have to go find them rather than just save them from an email that someone has sent you.

For example, let's say you bought a new TV and the instruction manual is online rather than printed out and included in the box. This is very common these days as more and more products don't come with manuals and would rather have you get them from their website. In order to view the manual, you will need to go to the manufacturer's website, find your TV model, and then find the manual that goes along with it. Unfortunately, not all websites work the same, and you will find that some are easier to use than others when it comes to getting what you are looking for.

For my example I want to find the manual for an RU8000 smart TV. So, I go to the manufacturer's website (in this case Samsung), find the downloads page, navigate to TVs, and then to the RU8000 model.

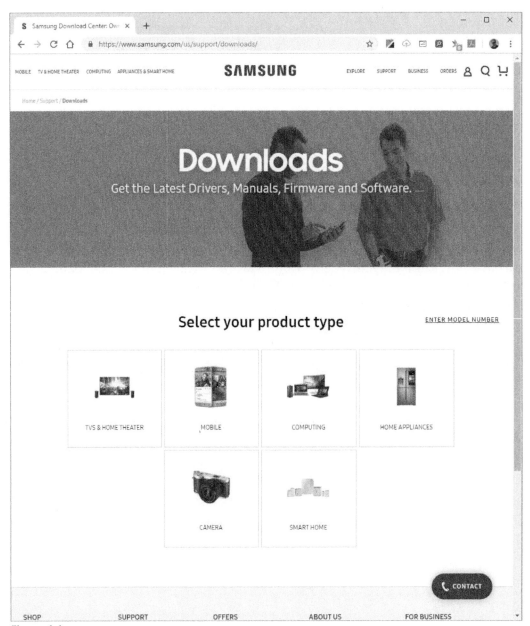

Figure 4.1

Figure 4.2 shows the download options for the RU8000 TV now that I have found my way to the correct model. I have an option to download firmware (a software update for my TV), or the manual, which is what I am looking for and has two available downloads.

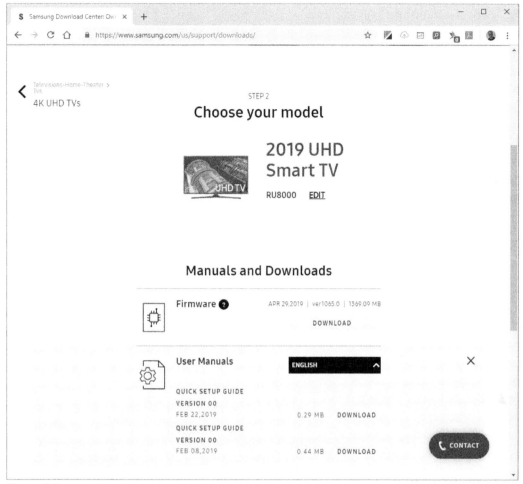

Figure 4.2

Next, I will choose the Feb 22, 2019 version (since it's newer) by clicking on the word DOWNLOAD next to it. Now this is where things can get a little tricky. Depending on what type of document you are downloading, your web browser might open it within the browser itself (like shown in figure 4.3), or you might be asked to download the file to your computer first. If it does open in your web browser but you want to have the actual manual on your computer, then we can use our right click options to take care of this.

Figure 4.3

Rather than left click on the DOWNLOAD link, I can right click on it and choose *Save as,* and then choose a location on my computer (figure 4.4). Another option is to use the *download* feature from the open document (as shown in figure 4.5) to save it to your computer. Unfortunately, the process for viewing and saving documents from websites is not going to be the same for every situation, so it will most likely take a little work on your end to figure out what needs to be done.

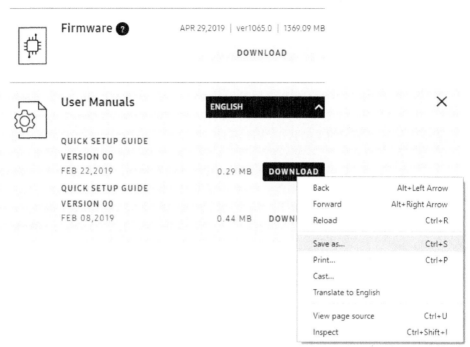

Figure 4.4

Figure 4.5

## FTP Sites

One way that people transfer files is via FTP sites that you can log into and either download files from, or upload files to. This is mostly used in a work situation rather than something you would do at home, and I will just go over the basics of how they work. There is a good chance you will never have to use an FTP site, but just in case you run into a situation at work where it's required, you can now at least have an idea of what they are talking about!

FTP stands for File Transfer Protocol, and is a method used by FTP sites to allow file transfers between two computers over the Internet. It can be done using a web browser, FTP client software, or even with a command prompt (which I won't even get into). If you plan on accessing FTP sites a lot, then you should think about installing an FTP client on your computer. There are many free ones out there such as Free FTP, Mozilla FileZilla, and my favorite, WinSCP.

Figure 4.6 shows an example of the WinSCP FTP client connected to an FTP site. On the left are the local files on my computer, and on the right are the remote files on the server\FTP site. All you need to do is drag and drop files or folders from one side to the other to transfer them back and forth.

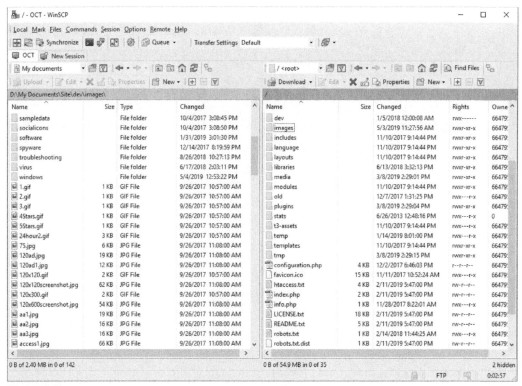

Figure 4.6

To access an FTP site with your web browser, you would simply enter the URL\address of that FTP site into the address bar of your browser and press enter on your keyboard. Then you will be prompted for a username and password to access the FTP site, and then you will be able to see the files and folders that you are allowed to download (figure 4.8). Having a username and password also applies to FTP clients when setting up the initial connection configuration.

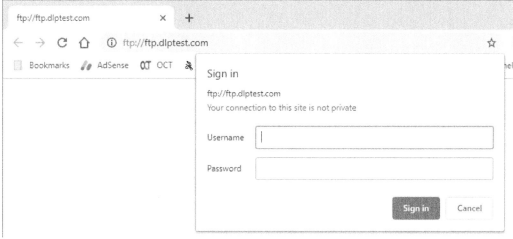

Figure 4.7

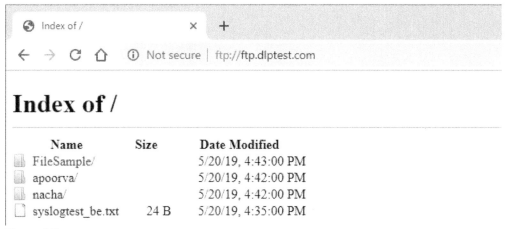

Figure 4.8

## Types of Software You Might Download

The Internet is a great place to get software that can be used on your computer for a variety of things such as video editing, word processing, games, and so on. Lots of the software you can find is free, or at least free to try for a limited amount of time. Just be careful when downloading any type of software from the Internet because scammers use this as a way to get into your computer. (I will go over how to stay safe in regards to downloading software in Chapter 9.)

You can find software the same way you find anything else online, and that is by doing a search for it. Then when you get to that website, you will usually find a download page where you can download the correct version of that software for your computer.

Since I will be talking about zip files in the next section, I will use the popular file compression software called WinZip as my example for downloading software. First I will do a search for WinZip in my search engine (the results of which are shown in figure 4.9). As you can see, the first result is an ad that was actually paid for by WinZip since their address (www.winzip.com) is next to it. I happen to know that www.winzip.com is their address, but you might not know for sure when looking at search results.

Figure 4.9

When you click on a link that is shown as an ad, you are costing that company money, so if you want to be nice, you can click on the non-ad result below the ad (if there is one) and save them a little money and maybe get yourself a little karma at the same time!

Next, I will click on the link that says *Download* and can also most likely click on the link that says *Download WinZip* and get the same result. Figure 4.10 shows the download page for the WinZip software. As you can see, there is a Windows version and a Mac version, so you would click on the link for whatever operating system your computer is running. Also notice how there is a *try it free* button and a *buy now* button. Clicking on the *try it free* button will let you download and install the software for free as a trail. These trials usually have time limits on them or don't include all of the functionality of the software.

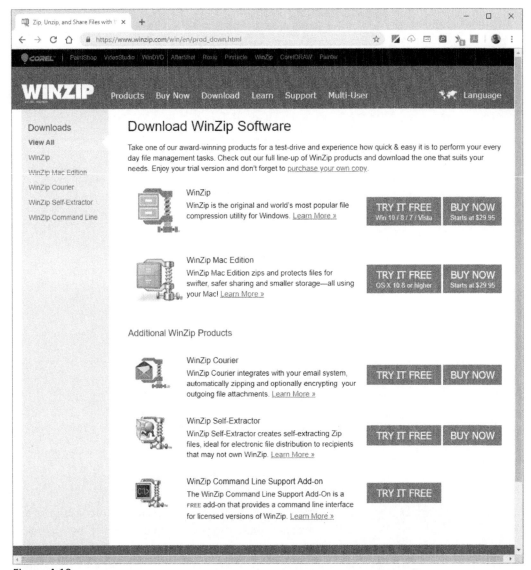

Figure 4.10

I will now click on the *try it free* button and download the trial of the software. When I do this, I am prompted to choose a location on my hard drive to save the installation file (winzip23-downwz.exe) to. In my case, I will put it in a folder called Downloads on my D drive.

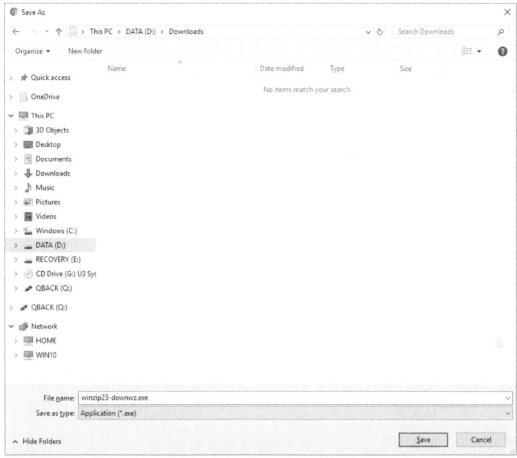

Figure 4.11

Figure 4.12 shows what the website looks like after downloading the file. Many times there will be a link you can click on to download the file again in case the download process failed or never started. Then, depending on what web browser you are using, you can many times access the downloaded file right from there. If you look at the bottom of figure 4.12 you will see the winzip23-downwz.exe file is shown at the bottom of the browser. From there you can do things like run the file to start the installation, or open the folder where you saved the file in (figure 4.13).

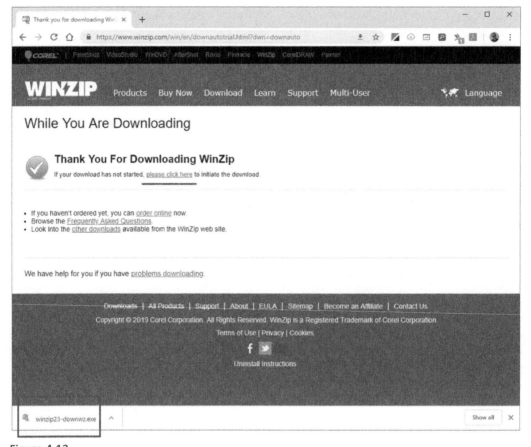

Figure 4.12

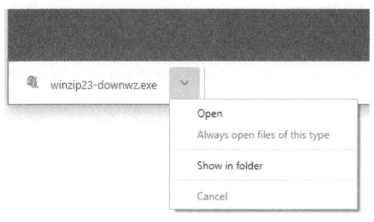

Figure 4.13

I know you are getting sick of hearing it, but the process for downloading software from the Internet will vary depending on where you are getting it from and what web browser you are using to download the software!

## Zip Files

Many times when you download a file or software from the Internet it will be in the form of a zip file. Zip files are used to compress files to make them smaller so they are easier and faster to download. It's often common to use zip files with email attachments so your files are not too large to email. Zip files are also used to combine multiple files into one file, which also makes things easier. Let's say you had 20 photos from your vacation that you wanted to send to someone. Rather than have 20 attachments in one email, you can "zip them up" into one file and send them as one attachment. Then the person on the other end can "unzip" them and have all 20 photos.

Most operating systems (Windows, Mac, etc.) have the ability to create zip files as well as extract files from zip files, so there is no real need to buy a separate program (such as WinZip that I mentioned before) unless you want to get into more advanced file compression methods. Figure 4.14 shows a zip file called *Auto Show.zip* on the left, and then the contents of that zip file with 20 pictures in it on the right.

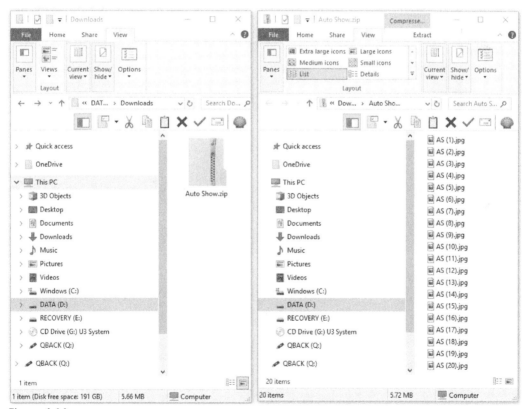

Figure 4.14

If you download some software that comes in a zip file, you should be able to just double click that zip file and then double click the file inside of it to start the installation program.

# Chapter 5 – Streaming Movies and Music

One of the most commonly performed activities that people do on the Internet is stream movies and music. With today's super-fast Internet speeds, it's easy to stream movies and TV shows in high quality HD format, as well as listen to all of your favorite music without having to break out the stereo system.

There are many upon many ways to get your favorite movies, TV shows, and music on your various devices, and trying to figure out what's best for you and your budget can get a little overwhelming. I would recommend using your newfound searching skills to see what's out there and find some real personal reviews to give you a better idea of what's best for you.

**Streaming Services & Devices**
I'm sure you have heard of services such as Netflix and Hulu for movies and TV and Pandora and Spotify for music, but there are many more services out there that offer similar content. You will need to decide if it's movies you are looking for, or just certain TV shows and find out what providers offer what you need. It's unlikely that you will find one service that offers everything you are looking for, so you will either need to make some sacrifices, or get more than one service subscription.

Another thing to consider is if the service you choose is supported on all of your devices and that there is either no limit, or a reasonable limit on how many of your devices you can access your account from. For example, if you sign up for a movie streaming service and it will only allow you to register five of your devices (computers, tablets, smartphones, etc.) and you have six devices, then you will not be able to watch movies on one of them.

You also need to make sure that all of the devices you want to use are supported by that streaming service. So, for example, if you sign up for Netflix, you should make sure there is a Netflix app for your tablet if you plan on using it on that device. For the most part, all major streaming services will work on all types of devices.

Computers and mobile devices are pretty straightforward to get working with streaming services because you generally either just go to their website or launch their app to get yourself going. But if you want to use your TV, then that can be a little more complicated. TVs can also have apps that are used to access online content, and if you have what they call a smart TV, then you should be ready to go—assuming you connected it to your wireless Internet connection at home. If not, then you will need to find the settings section on the TV, look for wireless or networking settings, and connect to your Wi-Fi connection just like you would with a computer or tablet. If you don't have the app for your service, then there is a good chance you can search for it and install it on your TV. Most newer Blu Ray players also have the capability to stream content as well if you don't have a smart TV.

There are also other specialty devices such as Roku adapters, Apple TV boxes, Amazon Fire boxes, and so on that you can attach to your TV and use to stream your content. They usually connect to an HDMI port on your TV just like your Blu Ray player would.

Figure 5.1

Just to get your research started, here is a list of some of the more popular movie, TV, and music streaming services. Some are free while others require a subscription.

- Netflix
- Amazon Prime Video
- HBO Go

- Hulu
- Sling
- Vevo
- Crackle
- iTunes
- Pandora
- Spotify
- Pluto TV
- iHeartRadio

## Bandwidth Considerations

Streaming movies and music requires data to travel back and forth between your device and where the movie or music is coming from. This back and forth action requires what is called bandwidth. Bandwidth is the amount of data that can be sent from one point to another in a certain period of time. The higher the quality of the movie you are viewing, the higher the bandwidth that will be required to get it to your device and have it be nice and clear.

Most home Internet connections are more than fast enough to handle HD movies and quality music streaming. However, if you are unlucky enough to be on a slow connection (such as satellite Internet because of your location), then you might suffer the consequences with lower quality images or having your movie pause to catch up with itself (this is called buffering).

If you watch your movies and TV outside the house, then there is a good chance you are using your cellular connection to stream unless you are somewhere such as a coffee shop or hotel where they provide a Wi-Fi connection. Using your cellular connection not only slows down your streaming speed, but can also increase your phone bill in a hurry if you go over your data limit. Of course, if you are on an unlimited plan, then you have nothing to worry about.

You should be able to find out what your home Internet connection speed is so you can see if you are ready to stream movies and music without any issues. It should be listed on your bill, or you can go to a speed testing website such as speedtest.net and it will tell you how fast your connection is. Figure 5.2 shows a speedtest.net test which will test your download and upload speeds. (You really only need to be concerned with the download speeds.)

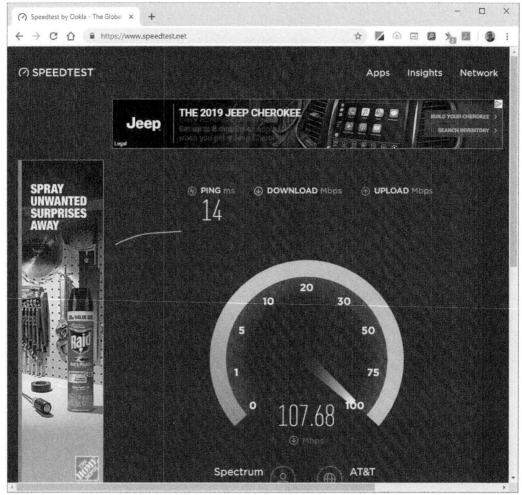

Figure 5.2

If you have at least a 25Mbps connection, then you should be fine for streaming movies and music, but of course more is always better! If you do upgrade, I don't think there is any real reason to pay for anything more than 100Mbps because you won't notice the difference except on your bill.

## YouTube and Other Video Sites
YouTube can technically be called a streaming site, but it's not the same as the others that I mentioned earlier because the videos that are available for viewing on YouTube are made by other Internet users such as yourself, and then uploaded to the site for others to watch. These videos can be as pointless as someone filming their cat sleeping, to something super informative such as a step by step tutorial on how to build a computer. Believe it or not, there are 300 hours of new videos uploaded to YouTube every minute!

YouTube does now have their own pay for streaming service called YouTube TV, and it offers content such as news, sports, and movie channels. Many of them are the same that you would get with your cable TV service, except you can watch these channels anywhere you have an Internet connection.

When you go to the YouTube website (www.youtube.com) you will see things like recommended and suggested videos that YouTube thinks you may like. These are based on previous videos you have watched if you have been there before. If not, then they will just suggest some trending videos for you to watch.

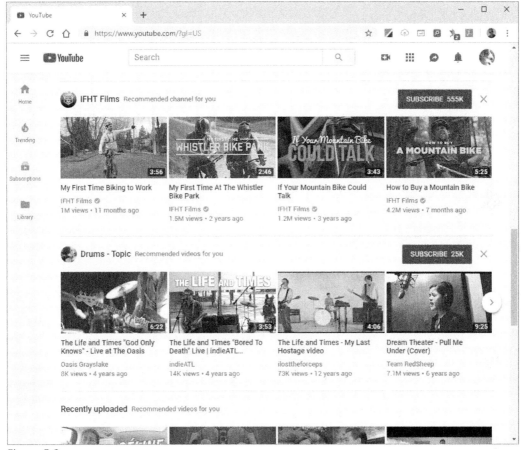

Figure 5.3

YouTube works the same way as a web browser where you type in a search for what you want to find. Figure 5.4 shows the results when I type in *dog tricks* for my search.

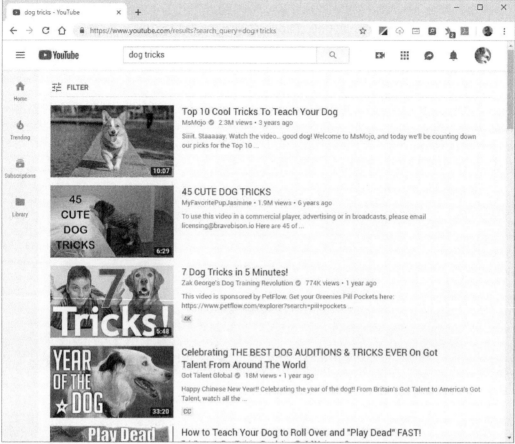

Figure 5.4

If you click on *Filter* at the top left, you will be able to tell YouTube how you want the results displayed and you can have it sort on things such as when it was uploaded, how long it is, or the quality of the video itself etc.

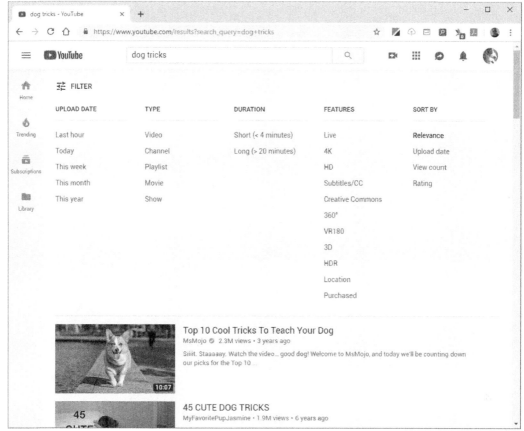

Figure 5.5

When you click on a video to play it, you will be given suggestions for recommended videos based on what you are watching on the right that you can also watch. Just be careful not to get stuck watching videos all day, because it's really easy to do!

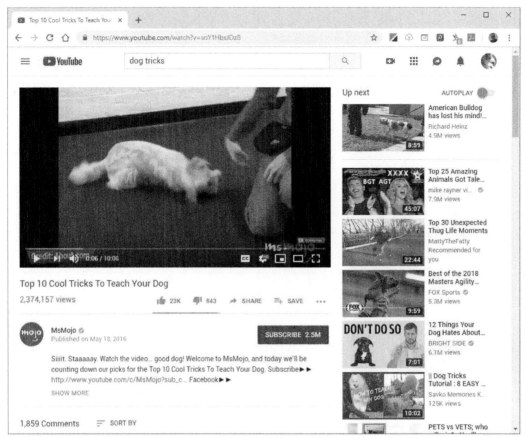

Figure 5.6

When you watch a video, you will notice several icons at the bottom of the video screen. Figure 5.7 shows you what each one does and it should be pretty self-explanatory. If you want to fast forward a video, you can simply put your mouse cursor on the video time location bar and move it forward or backward.

Figure 5.7

Figure 5.8 shows what each of the sections below the video are used for.

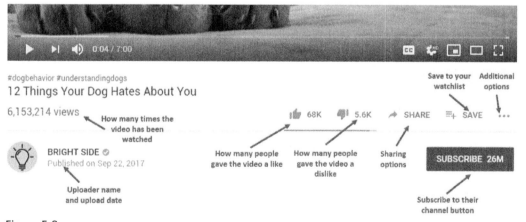

Figure 5.8

For the most part, these should be easy to understand, but I will go over a few that might not be so straight forward. The *Sharing* option will let you do things such as share the video on social media sites like Facebook and Twitter and also allow you to share it via email and with other methods depending on what type of device you happen to be on at the moment. The *Subscribe* button will add your YouTube account to that particular user's subscription list, and when they release new videos, you will be notified via email. The *Save* option lets you save the video to a watch list that you can go back to later and view it when you want. The three dots will give you other options such as reporting an inappropriate video or viewing a transcript of the audio in the video (as shown in figure 5.9).

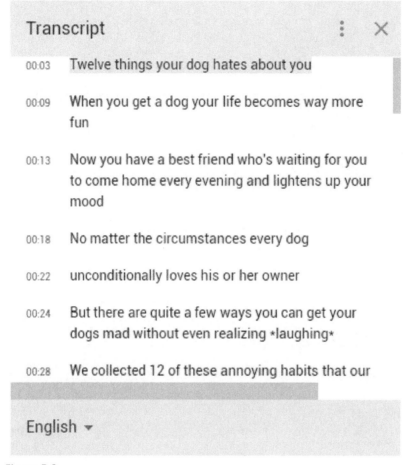

Figure 5.9

*Uploading to YouTube*

If you have a Google account, then you automatically have a YouTube account which will allow you to upload your own videos to the site and then you can share them with the world. If you are using a mobile device or have a webcam on your computer, you can also use the Go Live feature to live stream a video. Figure 5.10 shows the button you would click to upload a video using a web browser on your computer.

Figure 5.10

Once you click the button you simply browse to the location of the video file on your computer and start the upload process (figure 5.11). Then you will give the video a name and add a description. Underneath the description you can add what they call tags, which are labels used to describe what your video is about. They are used by YouTube to help others find your video based on them searching for similar words. The *visibility options* will let you make the video public or just private for you and others that you share the link with. The video won't go live until you click on the *Publish* button, even if it is 100% uploaded.

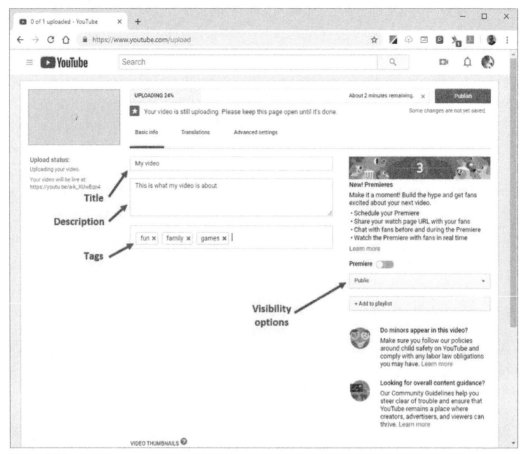

Figure 5.11

Once you have your video uploaded, you will be able to go into your video manager (or Creator Studio, as it's called) and do things like edit the video name and description, download your video, or even delete it. You can also see your viewing statistics from there.

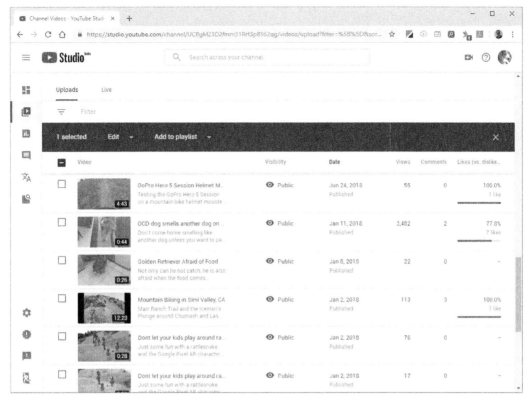

Figure 5.12

Of course, YouTube is not the only game in town, and there are other sites such as Vimeo, Dailymotion, and Metacafe. Sites like Vimeo offer pay-for plans that get you more features than YouTube does such as better quality playback, ad removal, custom logos, and so on. Plus, you will get different results for your searches. For example, if I enter *dog tricks* in the search box on the Dailymotion site, I get the results as shown in figure 5.13.

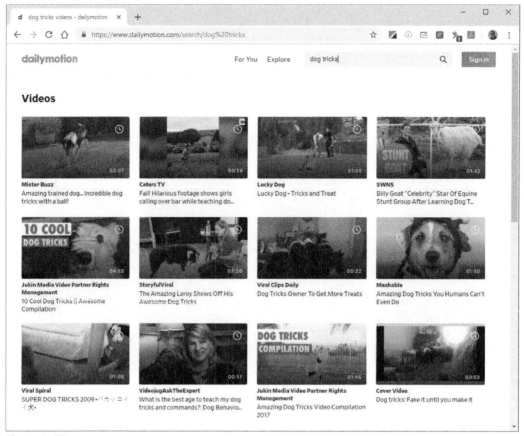

Figure 5.13

Then when you click on a video to watch, things look about the same as they do on YouTube with related videos and so on.

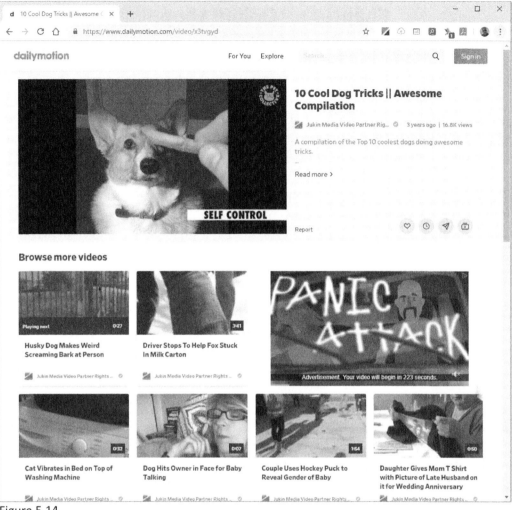

Figure 5.14

# Chapter 6 - Online Shopping

One of the best parts of the Internet is the ability to shop for pretty much anything you will ever need all from the comfort of your chair at home (or, for many, at the office!). There are so many ways to buy so many different types of things from around the world, and once you find them, you can have them shipped right to your door, sometimes the next day!

Thanks to online shopping, you no longer need to drive from store to store to find what you are looking for. Even if you plan on getting your item from a local store, you can still shop for it on their website and even buy it online and then pick it up at the physical store the same day. Or, if you want to send someone a gift, then you can ship the item directly to their house instead of yours.

Many physical stores will even price match with deals you find online, so if you would rather get your item locally but pay the online price, then that is one way to go. (For the most part, this is usually available with larger retailers, and the online price needs to be from a reputable site.)

## Popular Shopping Sites

There are many upon many online stores that offer anything you can imagine, but that doesn't mean that they are all the same and that you should whip out your credit card for the first one you come across. The more popular shopping sites are popular for a reason. They provide a wide selection at competitive prices while offering reliable shipping, secure transactions, and easy returns if necessary.

This doesn't mean that you should only stick to the more common shopping sites, but if you are new to online shopping, you might want to give them a try first since they tend to be run more professionally and easier to use. Plus, you can most likely get help from friends who have used the site as well since they are more commonly used.

### Amazon

The most popular shopping site of all at the moment is amazon.com, and they have been the most popular for many years now. You can find just about anything you need on Amazon and have it shipped to you in record time if you like. Since it's so popular, I will spend some time going over the site so if you decide to make an account for yourself or already have one, you will have a better idea of how to get around and make the most of your shopping experience.

Figure 6.1 shows the main Amazon website, and yours will not look exactly the same since the site changes constantly with new ads displayed and also products shown that are based on what Amazon thinks you may be interested in. One thing that *will* stay constant is the items on the top of that page that you use to navigate the site itself.

The first thing I want to point out at the upper left hand corner of the page is how in my example it says Amazon Prime. Prime is an additional service or subscription that you can sign up for that gives you benefits such as no minimum order for free shipping, free two day and even same day delivery, music streaming, free movies and TV shows, and so on. The cost of Prime is $119 per year or $12.99 per month. College students can get Prime Student for $59 per year (or $6.49 per month).

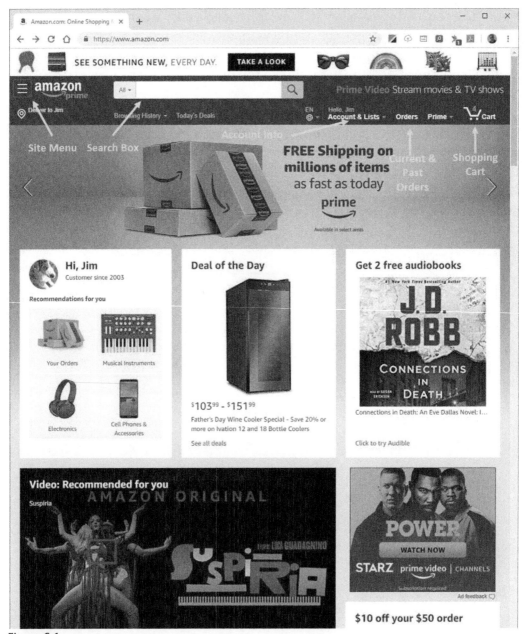

Figure 6.1

The Amazon site menu options can be accessed from the three horizontal bars in the upper left corner. From there, you will have many items to choose from such as searching for videos and music, searching for particular products, and browsing Amazon services. Take some time and go through the choices that sound interesting to you so you can get an idea of what you can do on the site.

Figure 6.2

The search bar works the same way it does when using a search engine like Google or Bing, but in this case you can only find things that are available on the Amazon website. If you do a search for something like *weather*, you most likely won't get the results you are looking for! Figure 6.3 shows the results when searching for blenders. As you can see, you get the results in the main section of the page and you will get many pages of results for an item as common as a blender. Fortunately, you can sort by price, customer reviews, and newest arrivals.

Figure 6.3

On the left hand side of the page, you will have other options to help narrow down your search. If you are a Prime member, you can have it only show results that are Prime eligible. Or you can narrow it down by department or brand if the results are too vague. I like how you can also have it show results based on their average customer review, so if you want to see blenders that have a four star rating or higher, for example, you can do that by clicking on the four star review section under *Avg. Customer Review*.

*Accounts and Lists* is where you can check your account settings and set preferences to enhance your shopping experience. For the most part, you won't do much in here, but if you need to do things like change your shipping address or email address you would do so from here. It's also where you will go to add or edit payment information such as stored credit cards.

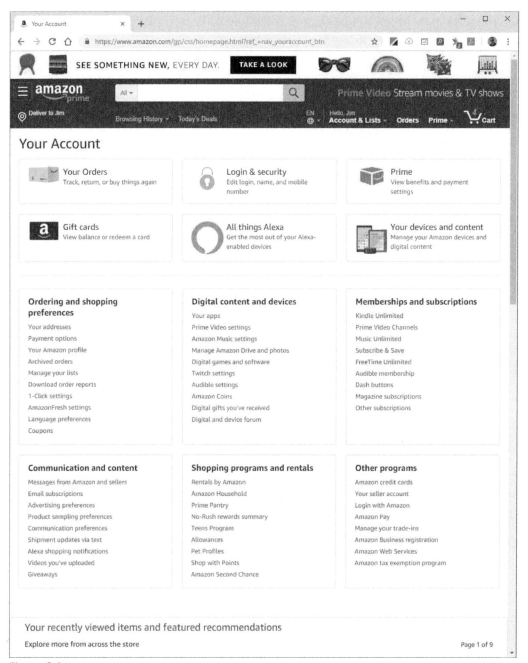

Figure 6.4

Amazon makes it really easy to track your orders and see what you have ordered in the past (which makes reordering items very easy). If you click on *Orders*, it will show you items that you have ordered that are in progress, as well as orders from the past that you have already received. Figure 6.5 shows that I have some items that were just delivered, and also shows that I have placed 93 orders in the past 6 months. I think I have a shopping problem!

If you look to the right of any one of the orders you will see that you have many options to choose from. You can track the package if it hasn't been delivered yet, as well as start the return process if you need to send a product back that you don't like or was defective. Once you have purchased an item, you are then allowed to write your own review for that item that others can read.

If you are looking for a particular item that you bought, then you can do a search for it using the *search all orders* box. This comes in handy if you want to reorder something again and want to make sure you get the exact same thing. Then you can click on the *Buy it again* button to reorder the item again.

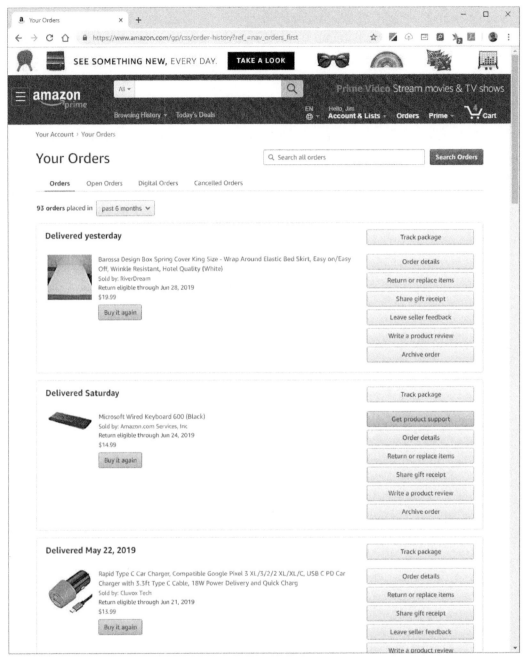

Figure 6.5

Clicking on *Open Orders* shows what orders I have in progress and when they are expected to arrive. If the items have not been shipped yet, then you have the option to cancel the order by clicking on the *Cancel items* button.

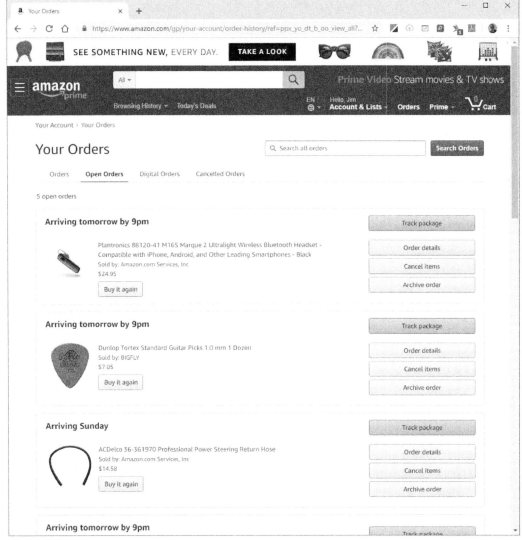

Figure 6.6

If you buy things like music, movies, or software from Amazon, you most likely will have the option to download these types of items directly to your computer so you don't need to wait for them to be delivered. Of course, that means you won't get the physical disk or case, but if you don't need it then this is the way to go. Once you download your order you can go to the *Digital Orders* section to view your purchases and download them again if needed (figure 6.7).

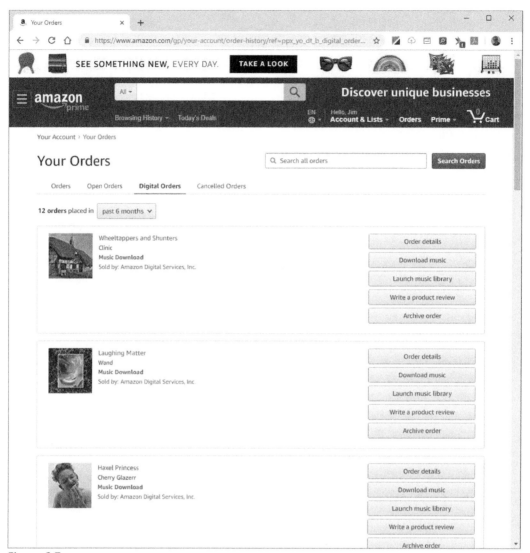

Figure 6.7

Figure 6.8 shows a product page for a blender that I have clicked on. As you can see, you get the description, pictures, and customer reviews for this particular item. It will also tell you the delivery timeframe so you have an idea of when you will get it if you order it. For many items on Amazon you have the option to buy it used, but use your better judgment when doing so, especially on electronics and other things that can stop working. For many items you can buy a protection plan to extend your warranty in case your item does decide to stop working on you.

There are two options when it comes to buying an item. If you click on *Add to Cart*, it will simply put that item in your virtual shopping cart and you can check out later and actually make the purchase. If you click on *Buy Now*, it will automatically make the purchase for you using your default shipping address and payment method and bypass the shopping cart.

If you do add an item to your cart, it will show up in the top right in the shopping cart icon (figure 6.9). Then you can click on the cart icon itself to go to your actual shopping cart (figure 6.10).

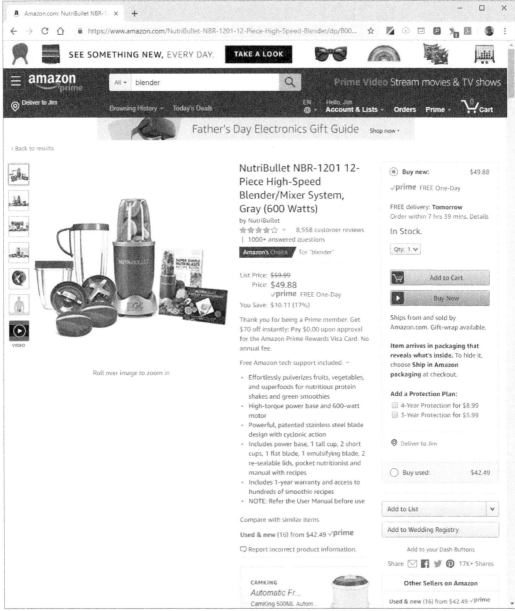

Figure 6.8

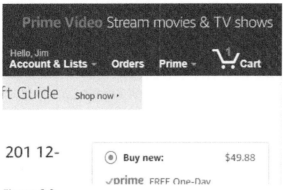

Figure 6.9

Take a look at the options underneath the item in the cart.  As you can see, you can delete the item from your cart, save it for later, or compare it with other items. The save it for later will just move it out of your cart and put it underneath so you can still have it around in case you want to move it back to your cart. As you can see in figure 6.10, I have some items in my *saved for later* area.

Chapter 6 - Online Shopping

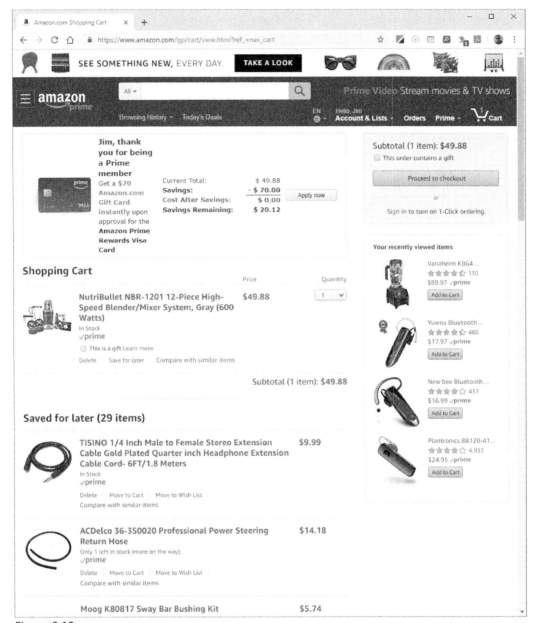

Figure 6.10

When you are ready to buy the items in your cart simply click on the *Proceed to checkout* button and you will see a screen similar to figure 6.11. Then you can confirm your shipping address, payment method, and the items and quantities to be shipped. If you have an Amazon gift card, you can enter the card number under *payment method* to have the gift card amount subtracted from your total.

Section 3 shows your delivery options. Since I have Prime, I can get it delivered to me as early as tomorrow. Sometimes if you want an item faster you will have a choice to pay for expedited shipping if the faster shipping option is not available.

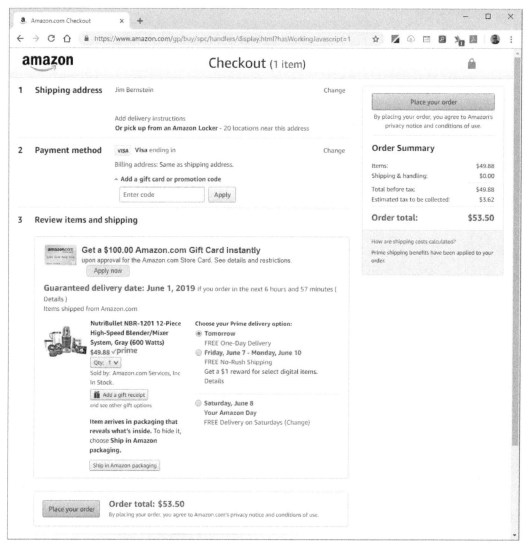

Figure 6.11

If everything looks good, then you can click on the *Place your order* button and then you will be given a confirmation screen that you can review for accuracy. You will also get an email confirmation as well.

*eBay*

eBay has been around since 1995 and is a great way to find deals on new and used products. It's a little trickier to use than Amazon because many items are sold auction style where you bid on them and the item goes to the highest bidder after the set auction time is complete. Many listings will have what they call a *Buy it now* price where you can just buy a product without having to worry about bidding on it. Another neat feature of eBay is the *make an offer* feature where you can make an offer on an item that is lower than its listing price and see if the seller accepts your offer. Plus, if you have something to sell, then you can do that here much easier than you can do on Amazon.

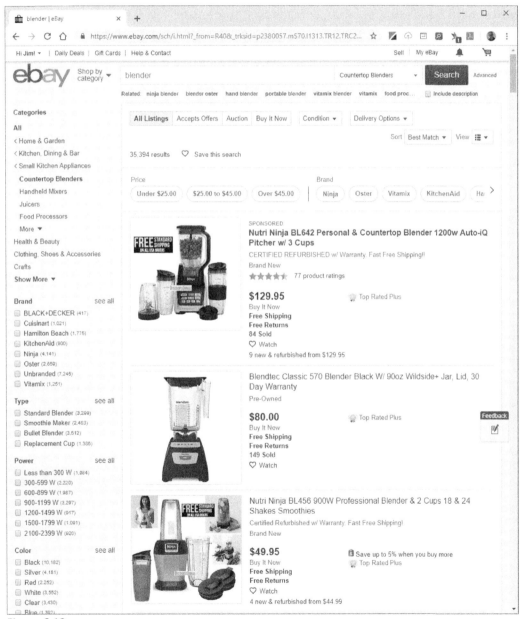

Figure 6.12

As you can see in figure 6.12, the shopping interface is similar to that of Amazon where you have your search results in the center and ways to narrow down these results on the left hand side of the screen. Notice on the top how there are options to display results that accept offers, are up for auction, are new or used, and so on.

Once you click on an item you will get a lot of information about that item and the person or company selling it. In figure 6.13 I highlighted some of the information you should be looking at when considering purchasing a product from eBay. One thing to watch out for is to make sure the product you are buying is new and not refurbished (unless you are okay with saving some money by not buying a brand new one).

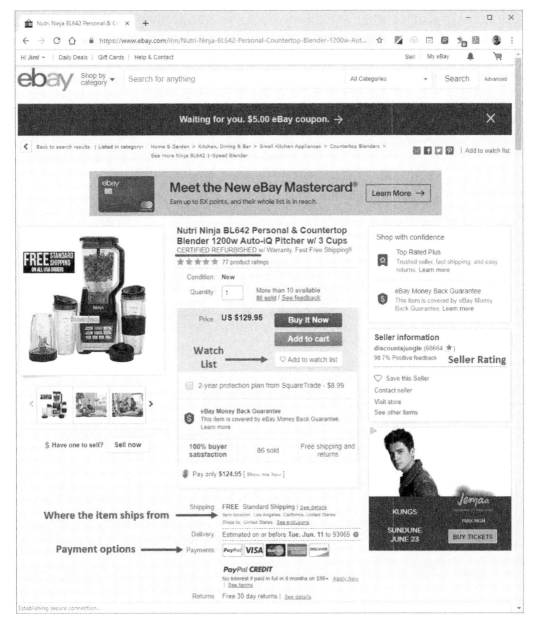

Figure 6.13

You should always look at the seller rating when buying on eBay since many times you are buying from an individual person rather than an actual business. If their rating is too low or they have a lot of complaints, then you might want to consider buying the item from someone else.

When it comes to how soon you will get your product, you should look at where it is shipping from. If you need it soon and it's coming from another country, then that will most likely take longer to get to you. For the most part, you can get pretty accurate arrival dates when you enter your shipping information so you will know when to expect your item.

eBay takes most popular payment methods such as VISA, MasterCard, and Discover, but this will vary depending on who you buy the items from. Many eBay users like to use PayPal because it sends them the money directly to their PayPal account. (I will be going over PayPal later in this chapter.)

Many times the price of a product will drop (for example, if they are having trouble selling them). If you click on the *Add to watch list* button you can have eBay keep an eye on the price so that you will be notified when the price changes in case you don't mind waiting for a better deal.

When you are ready to buy and click on the *Add to cart* button, you might get prompted to add a protection plan to your purchase. I generally don't do this, but it's up to you if you want to pay for some peace of mind or not.

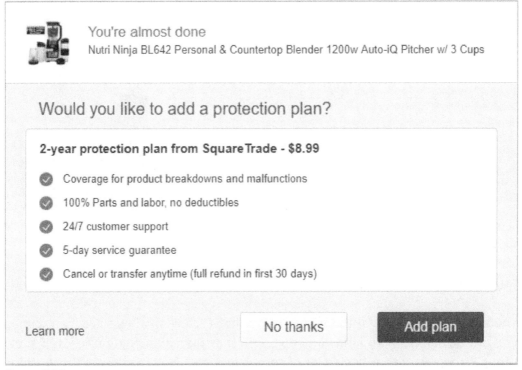

Figure 6.14

Then after that, all you need to do is make sure your shipping address is correct and choose your payment method and you will be ready to go.

*Craigslist*

Although I really wouldn't call Craigslist a shopping site, it might be something you are interested in using to find deals on used items ranging from furniture to electronics to cars. It's also a useful place to find things such as housing, services, and jobs. Craigslist was founded in 1995 by Craig Newmark to be used for the San Francisco Area and over time expanded to cover just about any area of the country you can imagine.

Craigslist works by allowing anyone the option to post goods and services for sale and then others can contact that person if they are interested in the goods or services. Since anyone can make an account to sell things, you need to be careful when using Craigslist because you never know who will be showing up at your door to buy something you are selling, or you never know who will be opening up their door when you go to someone's house to buy something. It's best to meet at a public location if possible, and if you are selling something from home try and have it out front or in your garage so the buyer doesn't have to come inside your house.

To use Craigslist, all you need to do is go to their site and choose your location. Figure 6.15 shows the Craigslist site for Bellingham WA, and this will look the same no matter what location you are browsing.

Figure 6.15

As you can see there are many categories to choose from, and all you need to do is select what category you wish to browse or do a search from the search box in the upper left hand corner. Once again, I am going to look for my blender, so when I type in *blender* from the search box I get the results shown in figure 6.16.

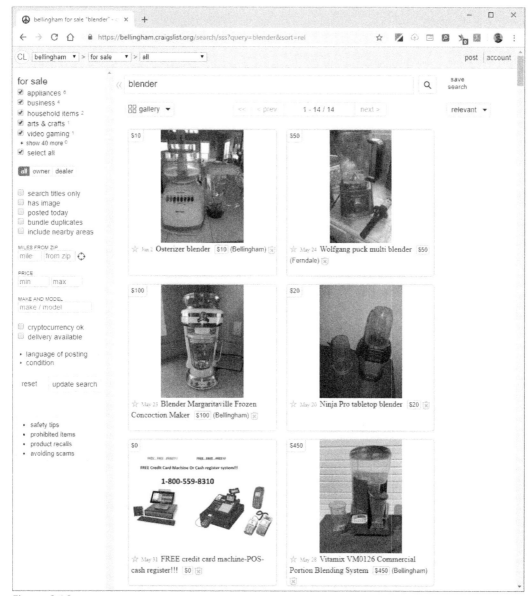

Figure 6.16

Once again, you will see the results in the middle of the page and have options on the left to narrow down your search results. When you click on a result you will get more details on that item (as shown in figure 6.17).

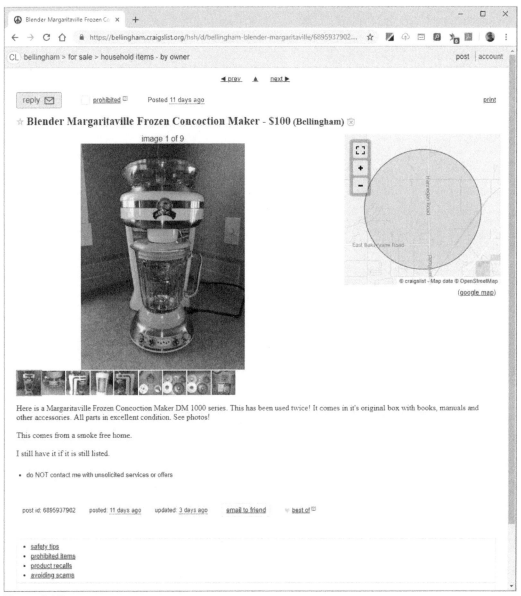

Figure 6.17

Here you can get things like a description, additional pictures, and a general location of the item on a map. If you wish to inquire about the item then you can click on the reply button on the top left to send that person a message (figure 6.17). Some people will put their phone numbers in the ad so you can call or text them, but for the most part people will use email for communication purposes. Craigslist offers a way of "masking" your real email address when posting an ad with a craigslist email address so you don't end up putting your real email address online for all to see. This is shown in figure 6.18 at the top under *reply by email*.

◄ prev ▲ next ►

Figure 6.18

Once you start an email conversation with a Craigslist seller you will simply use your email program to go back and forth like you would if you were emailing a friend.

To sell on Craigslist you will need to make a free account, and then you can start posting ads of your own. When you click on Post, you will have some options as to what you want to sell (figure 6.19).

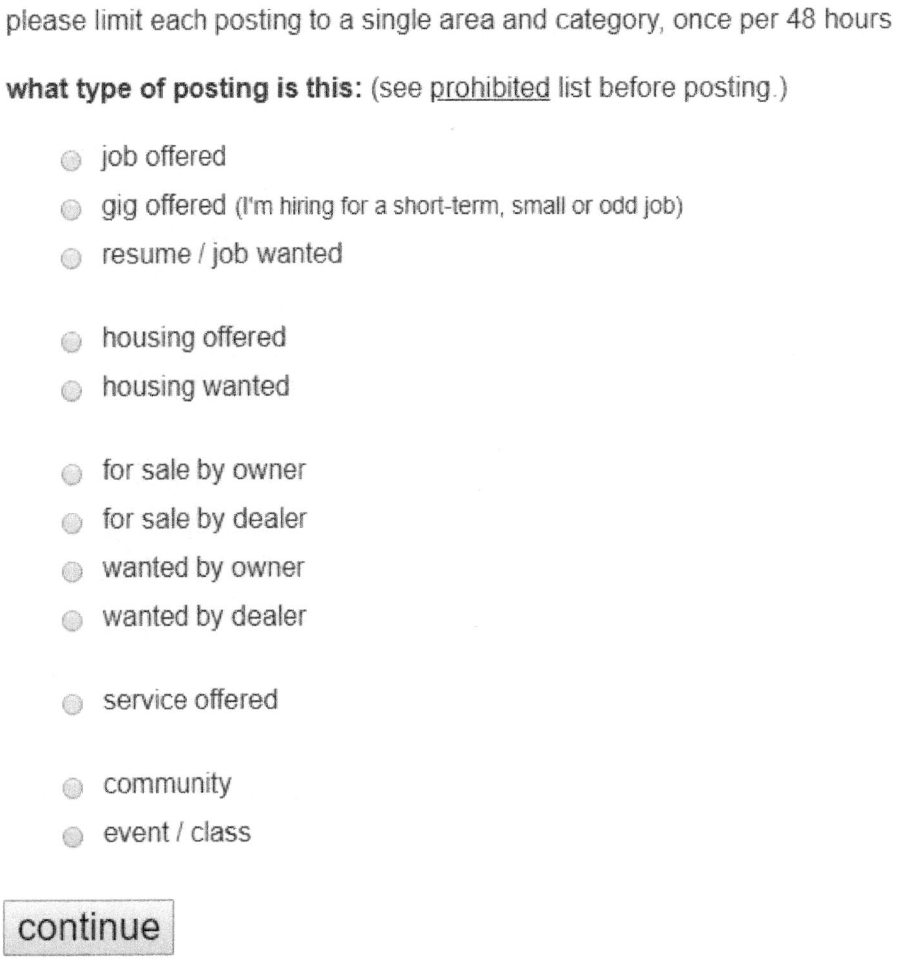

please limit each posting to a single area and category, once per 48 hours

**what type of posting is this:** (see prohibited list before posting.)

- job offered
- gig offered (I'm hiring for a short-term, small or odd job)
- resume / job wanted

- housing offered
- housing wanted

- for sale by owner
- for sale by dealer
- wanted by owner
- wanted by dealer

- service offered

- community
- event / class

| continue |

Figure 6.19

For my example I will sell my old blender to make space for my new one and click the option that says *for sale by owner,* and then click on the *continue* button. Out of the long list of categories I will then choose *appliances – by owner.*

**please choose a category:** (see <u>prohibited</u> list and <u>recall information</u> before posting.)

- ⊙ antiques - by owner
- ⊙ appliances - by owner
- ⊙ arts & crafts - by owner
- ⊙ atvs, utvs, snowmobiles - by owner
- ⊙ auto parts - by owner
- ⊙ auto wheels & tires - by owner
- ⊙ aviation - by owner
- ⊙ baby & kid stuff - by owner (no illegal sales of <u>recall items</u>, e.g. drop-side cribs, <u>recalled strollers</u>)
- ⊙ barter
- ⊙ bicycle parts - by owner
- ⊙ bicycles - by owner
- ⊙ boat parts - by owner
- ⊙ boats - by owner
- ⊙ books & magazines - by owner
- ⊙ business/commercial - by owner
- ⊙ cars & trucks - by owner (<u>FAQ</u>) ($5 per post)
- ⊙ cds / dvds / vhs - by owner (no pornography please)
- ⊙ cell phones - by owner
- ⊙ clothing & accessories - by owner
- ⊙ collectibles - by owner
- ⊙ computer parts - by owner
- ⊙ computers - by owner

Figure 6.20

Then I will fill in the details about my blender along with the brand, condition, and price. (You don't have to fill in all the sections of the posting details if you don't know them or if they don't apply.) The section that says *CL mail relay (recommended)* is where craigslist will mask your email address with one of their own, so I suggest you always use this option. I don't recommend putting your phone number or address unless you want extra sales calls during dinner time!

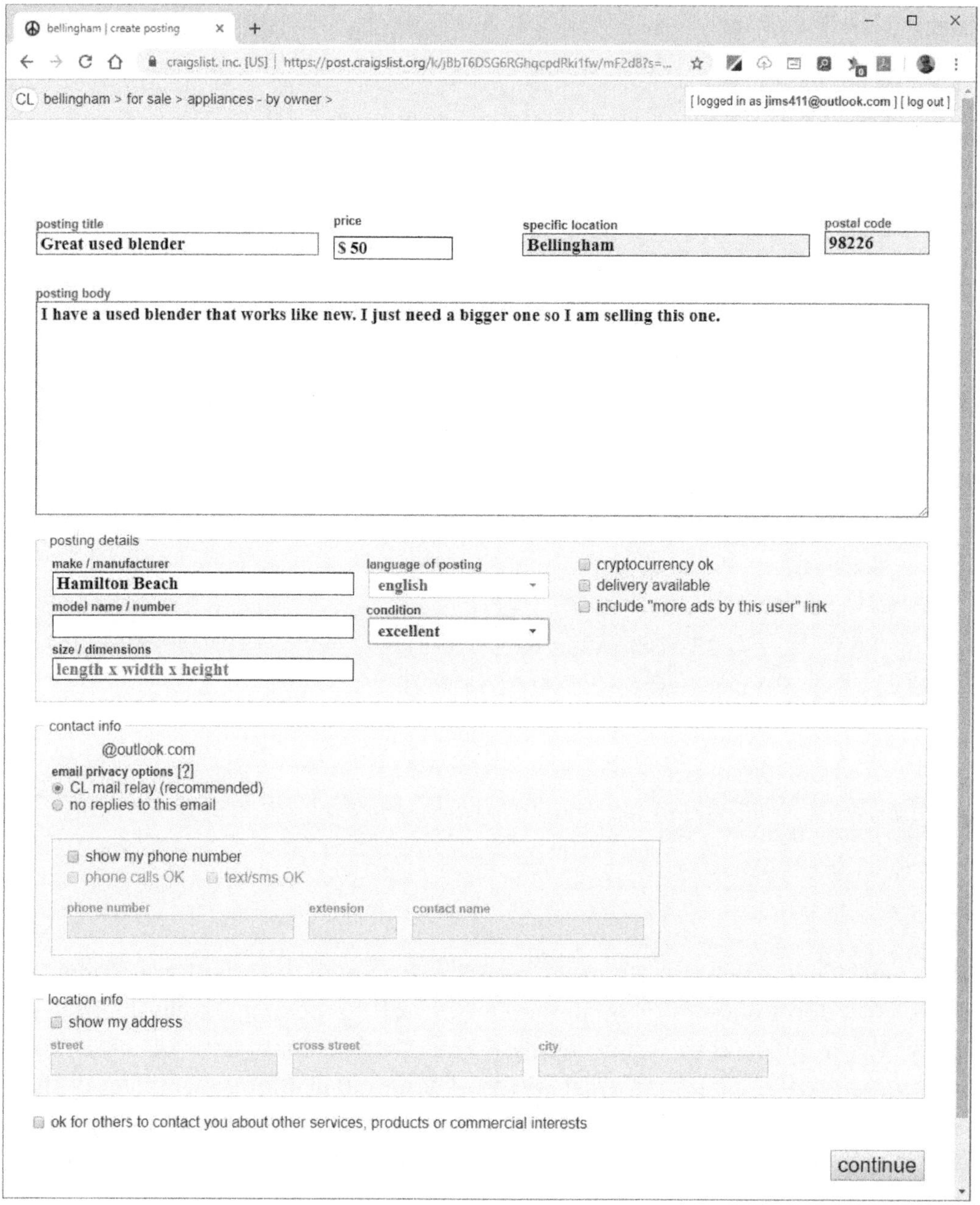

Figure 6.21

Next, you can drag the circle on the map to show the general location of where the person would have to go to look at or buy your item.

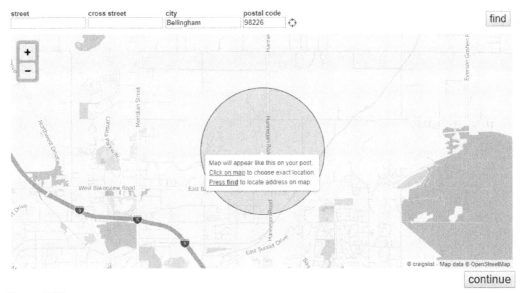

Figure 6.22

Next, you can add pictures of your item and decide which one will be the featured picture that will show as the main image for your ad.

Figure 6.23

Then after everything looks good, you can publish your ad and wait for people to contact you about buying your item.

Figure 6.24

Notice at the top of figure 6.24 that it says the ad will expire in 45 days. One thing you should do when posting Craigslist ads it to go into your account and view your postings every few days. If you see a link that says *renew*, you should click on it so it puts your ad back on top of the search results.

*Other Sites*

There are many upon many other shopping sites online, and some are dedicated to specific products such as electronics or clothing while others offer products from just about any category. Rather than go through more examples from other sites that will look similar to the previous examples, I will just give you a listing of some of the more popular online shopping sites that you can check out for yourself.

- Etsy.com
- Target.com
- Walmart.com
- Wish.com
- BestBuy.com
- HomeDepot.com

Don't forget that you can also shop from your search engine search results like I briefly discussed earlier in this book. So, for example, if I were to search for blenders in Google, I would see the shopping results as seen in figure 6.25. The main difference will be that the results will be from various shopping sites around the globe and not just from one online retailer. If you look at the first result, you can see that under the item title it says *from 50+ stores*, meaning Google found that particular blender for sale from over 50 online retailers.

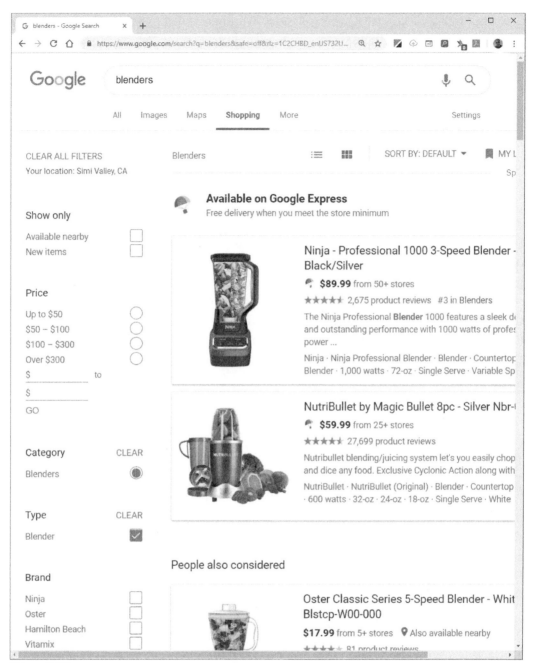

Figure 6.25

## Product Reviews

When shopping online or even at your local store, it's nice to be able to find out what experiences other shoppers have had who have purchased the same product that you are interested in buying. Most sites will offer its customers the opportunity to post a review of the product they have bought so that other customers can hear their thoughts on things like the quality of the product, shipping time, and so on.

Product reviews are not what they used to be, and by that I mean you can't trust them as much as you could in the old days. Many companies find ways to alter these overall ratings by doing things such as paying others to post fake reviews or using other mischievous methods. This doesn't mean *all* reviews are fake, but when you see a bunch of five star reviews along with a bunch of one star reviews, it makes you wonder how that product can have that many reviews on both sides of the scale. What I like to do is look at the three and four star reviews to hopefully get the most honest reviews. Of course, many of the five star reviews are valid as well, so it doesn't hurt to read those. I also find that many of the one star reviews are from people who just like to hear themselves complain or had a bad experience that was just a fluke or has nothing to do with the product itself (such as a box that was damaged during shipping).

For my review example I will go back to Amazon, pick another blender, and show you the reviews for it. Figure 6.26 shows that this blender has 3,355 customer reviews, which is quite a lot of reviews in general. If you look at the stars it shows that the average review rating for this blender is about 4.5 stars.

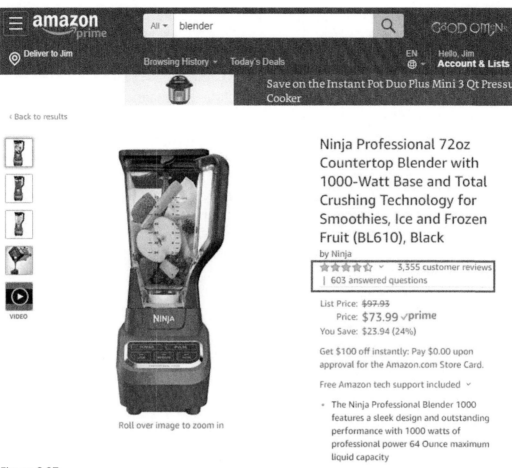

Figure 6.27

Clicking on the down arrow next to the stars will show you the percentage that each star has towards the total rating. If you look at figure 6.28, you will see that 71% of the reviewers gave it a five star rating.

Figure 6.28

Clicking on See all 3,355 reviews will allow you to dig deeper into the reviews and sort or filter the results (figure 6.29). If you want to see all of the one star reviews, for example, then you can click where it says 1 star and see only those results (figure 6.30).

Ninja Professional 72oz Countertop Blender with 1000-Watt Base and... › Customer reviews

## Customer reviews

 3,355

4.3 out of 5 stars ˅

# Ninja Professional 72oz Countertop Blen...

by Ninja

Price: $73.99 ✓prime

| | |
|---|---|
| 5 star | 71% |
| 4 star | 9% |
| 3 star | 5% |
| 2 star | 4% |
| 1 star | 11% |

Write a review

---

### Top positive review

See all 2,698 positive reviews ›

tallslenderguy

★★★★☆ owned 6 weeks
January 5, 2018

I'm a healthcare professional and bought this after researching the competition (i.e., "Vita-Mix"). After reading through a gazillion comments and reviews (including CR who rates the Ninja #2) I opted for the lower priced Ninja. I have used mine twice a day for the 6 weeks I have owned it, I use it for making smoothies. I blend for health, I have a morning fruit and berry smoothie and I have an afternoon veggie
Read more

992 people found this helpful

### Top critical review

See all 657 critical reviews ›

Leah McFaul

★☆☆☆☆ But this is such a horrible blender for what you pay
March 28, 2018

I never write reviews. But this is such a horrible blender for what you pay, I had to write a review. Another reviewer wrote "it takes the smooth out of smoothie" and he couldn't be more right. I'm not sure how this blender got so many good reviews. So many times I tried making my smoothies and açaí bowls and had to stick a spoon in the blender and
Read more

239 people found this helpful

---

🔍 Search customer reviews        Search

**SORT BY**        **FILTER BY**

Top rated ˅    All reviewers ˅    All stars ˅    Text, image, ... ˅

Figure 6.29

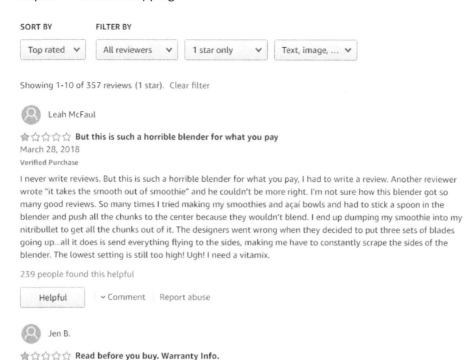

SORT BY          FILTER BY

| Top rated ⌄ | All reviewers ⌄ | 1 star only ⌄ | Text, image, ... ⌄ |

Showing 1-10 of 357 reviews (1 star).   Clear filter

Leah McFaul

★☆☆☆☆  **But this is such a horrible blender for what you pay**
March 28, 2018
Verified Purchase

I never write reviews. But this is such a horrible blender for what you pay, I had to write a review. Another reviewer wrote "it takes the smooth out of smoothie" and he couldn't be more right. I'm not sure how this blender got so many good reviews. So many times I tried making my smoothies and açaí bowls and had to stick a spoon in the blender and push all the chunks to the center because they wouldn't blend. I end up dumping my smoothie into my nitribullet to get all the chunks out of it. The designers went wrong when they decided to put three sets of blades going up...all it does is send everything flying to the sides, making me have to constantly scrape the sides of the blender. The lowest setting is still too high! Ugh! I need a vitamix.

239 people found this helpful

| Helpful |       ⌄ Comment  |  Report abuse |

Jen B.

★☆☆☆☆  **Read before you buy. Warranty Info.**
November 16, 2017
Verified Purchase

I wanted to really like this product based on all the positive reviews I read. I bought it in August, and now it's November and the pitcher has cracked. I used it may be once a week to blend smoothies. The pitcher is not covered by their 1 year warranty, which is ridiculous, like it's an extra part or something. To return the product you have to pay $19.99. Is it worth it? You decide for yourself.

158 people found this helpful

| Helpful |       ⌄ 1 comment  |  Report abuse |

 girlinpinkwaders

★☆☆☆☆  **Blender jar exploded!**
July 23, 2017

I've had my Ninja for about 18 months. I loved it. Used primarily for smoothies with frozen fruit. The other day it exploded on me and tore a hole through it. I have contacted Ninja. They didn't seem too concerned about it, and when I pressed them and offered to send them the defective blender jar so they could figure out the defect, they didn't seem very interested. The email they gave me was incorrect so I have to call them again to try and pursue this. I don't want another one, I just want them check it out because obviously there is an issue.

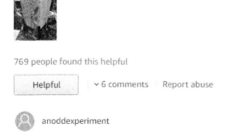

769 people found this helpful

| Helpful |       ⌄ 6 comments  |  Report abuse |

anoddexperiment

★☆☆☆☆  **It cracks and leaks!**

Figure 6.30

So be sure to read reviews when shopping online for things, especially if they are costly items, to see what other people think. If you are buying something you have bought before and know you like it, then you can pretty much ignore what others have to say. Just try not to make your decision based solely on what other people think because you might miss out on a great product that would have worked out just fine for you.

## Secure Payment Methods

When buying products online, you want to have the safest experience possible so you don't end up getting ripped off or have your personal information stolen etc. I will be going over online safety in Chapter 9, but for now I just wanted to go over some key concepts when it comes to staying secure when paying for your purchases.

The most important thing to consider when shopping online is to make sure you are shopping on a safe and reputable site to begin with. If the site looks like it was designed by a child and has spelling and grammar errors, then it might be something you want to stay away from. Or, if it's based out of another country that might not be known for its security, then that's another red flag.

One of the most important things to check for when shopping online is that you are on the site you are supposed to be on and that it's a secure website. Anyone can make a website that looks just like amazon.com, but if the address bar doesn't say amazon.com, then you know something is wrong. You also want to make sure that there is an S at the beginning of the address where it says *https*. If it just says http, then it's not a secure website and you shouldn't be shopping there. Figure 6.31 shows that I am on the amazon.com website and that it's a secure site so I can feel comfortable giving my credit card information to them.

Figure 6.31

Speaking of credit cards, many sites offer you the opportunity to save your shipping and credit card information on the site so you don't need to type in each time you want to buy something. If it's a site you will be using often, then you might want to save your information, but if it's going to be a one-time thing, then

I would advise against it. I also wouldn't save debit card information on a site in case your debit card doesn't have the same type of fraud protection that most credit cards have.

**PayPal**

There are other ways to pay for items online besides giving them your credit card. Many sites these days will use payment services that allow you to pay them directly from your bank account and bypass using your credit card. One of the most popular online payment services is called PayPal.

PayPal allows you to create an account and link it directly to your bank account to make purchases online. You can keep a balance in your PayPal account if you like, or if you don't have any money in your account it will take it directly from your bank account. You can also link a credit card to your PayPal account if you desire.

When you choose the PayPal payment option on a site it will take you to the PayPal login page where you will sign in with your username and password that you set up your account with, and then approve the transaction. Then it will take you back to the site where you are buying the item from and allow you to finish the transaction. It's as simple as that!

You can also log into the PayPal site at any time to see things like your balance and recent transactions. If you take a look at figure 6.32 you will see that you get a lot of information right from the Summary page of your account. You can see things like the balance in your account and also the balance in your PayPal Credit account (if you have signed up for one). The PayPal Credit account is like a credit card, so any money that shows up there is money you owe, not money you have to spend!

At the bottom of the page you will see what bank accounts or credit cards you have linked to your PayPal account. Keep in mind that if you change or cancel one of these accounts, then you will have to update the information in PayPal with your new accounts in order to use them with PayPal.

If you have previously sent someone money they will show up in the *Send again* section, which is more like a recent transaction section that makes it easy to send that person more money.

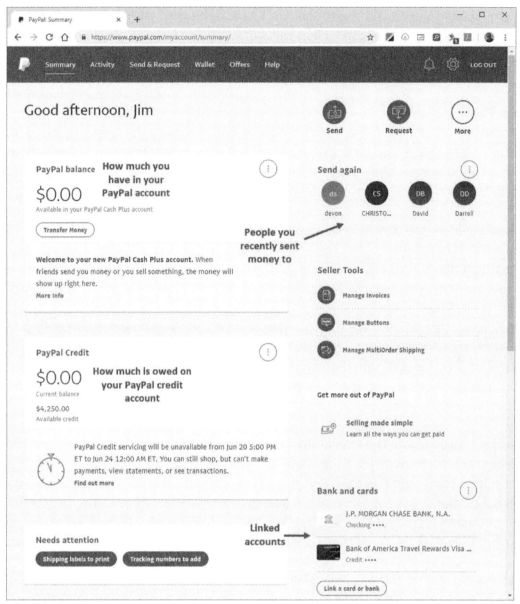

Figure 6.32

Figure 6.33 shows the Activity page where you can see all of the money you have sent and received via PayPal. You can enter in a date range as well if you want to only see results from a certain time period.

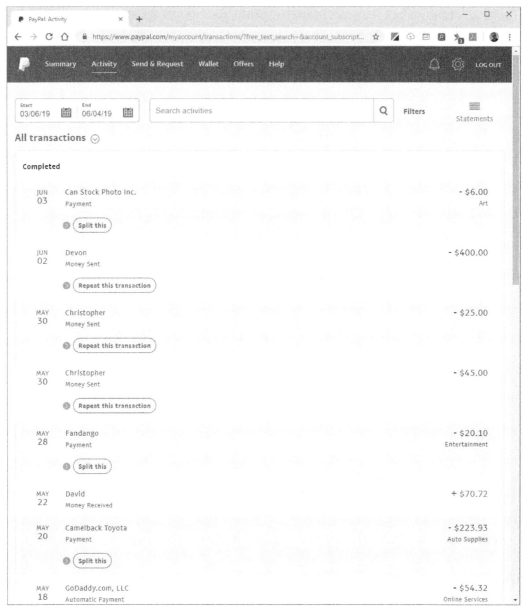

Figure 6.33

One of the great benefits of PayPal is that you can use it to send other people money rather than doing something like sending a check, getting cash out of the ATM, or doing a bank transfer. This also comes in handy for buying things from sites such as Craigslist because you most likely won't be able to use a credit card, and if you use cash then you have no record of the transaction in case there is a problem.

There are two ways to send money to other people via PayPal. You can do the friends and family method, which lets you send money for free, or you can use the pay for item or service method, which will result in a charge for the person on the receiving (selling) end. When you use the pay for item or service method, you get protection from PayPal on your purchase in case you don't get the item after you pay or it's defective. It's not a 100% guarantee that you will be taken care of, but it's a lot better than having no protection at all.

When you click on the Send & Request section you can enter that person's email account or phone number that they have associated with their PayPal account. You will need to ask them what address or number to use because you can't just put in anything you like and expect it to work unless it's associated with their PayPal account.

## Send money to anyone

Name, email or number
Jim@sendmemoney.com

Next

How it works ?

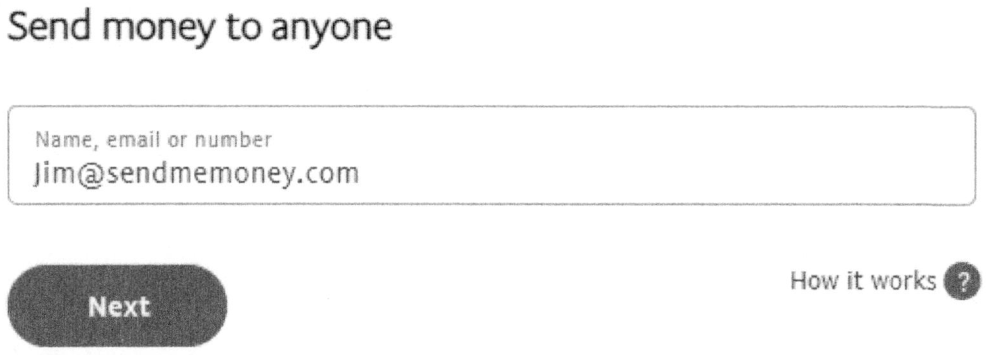

Figure 6.34

Then you will be asked if you are sending to a friend or paying for an item or a service (figure 6.35). If you are sending to someone you trust, then you will use the friend option so they don't get charged for the transaction. When I say get charged, I mean that PayPal will take a small percentage out of the transaction for themselves. The fee for each transaction is $0.30 plus 2.9% of the amount they are receiving.

# What's this payment for?

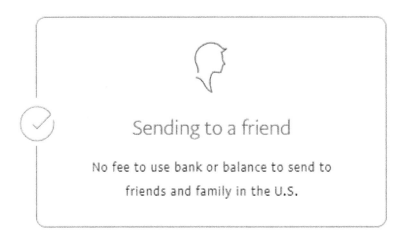

### Sending to a friend

No fee to use bank or balance to send to
friends and family in the U.S.

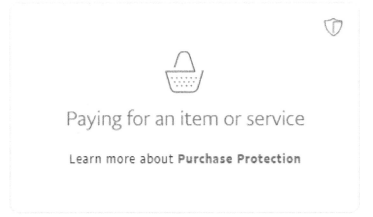

### Paying for an item or service

Learn more about **Purchase Protection**

Figure 6.36

PayPal is free to use and has been a safe and effective way to pay for online purchases and for sending people money. It's easy to sign up for, and all you need to do to link your checking account is put in your account number and routing number off one of your checks and you are good to go!

# Chapter 7 – Online Applications and Services

These days the Internet is used for much more than searching for cute dog pictures and shopping for blenders, which is fine if that's all you care about! But if you want to do more with the Internet, then there are some other tools you can use to make the most productive use of your time. In fact, many businesses run their entire operation online and don't even have a physical location.

## Office Applications

I'm sure you have used programs like Microsoft Word or Excel at work or at home and are familiar with how they work and what they are meant to be used for. And FYI, Microsoft is not the only game in town when it comes to these types of programs, but they are the biggest player! Just a few short years ago in order to use these types of programs, you would need to install them on each computer that you wanted to run them on and also have a software license for each one.

These days you can now run your office productivity programs online via your web browser and the Internet. There are several online services that let you run the same types of programs on just about any device that you can connect to the Internet with. But instead of calling them "programs", they usually refer to them as "applications" or "apps" for short.

 When using these types of applications on smartphones and tablets, you usually need to install an app on that device to be able to run it. When using these applications on your desktop computer, you will most likely only need to use your web browser and not have to install any additional software.

Rather than go over all of the available apps you can use to do things such as create documents, spreadsheets, and presentations, I will just go over a couple of the most popular ones, which are Microsoft Office 365 and Google Docs since they are at the top of the list when it comes to popularity and functionality.

Office 365 is a subscription-based service from Microsoft that will allow you to use their online applications for a fee. They do have a free version called Microsoft Office Online, which doesn't have all the bells and whistles of Office 365, but will probably do the job just fine for many users. As you can see in figure 7.1, Office Online has many built-in apps for things besides documents and spreadsheets such as an email client, calendar, and contact manager. They even offer free online file storage, which I will get to later in this chapter.

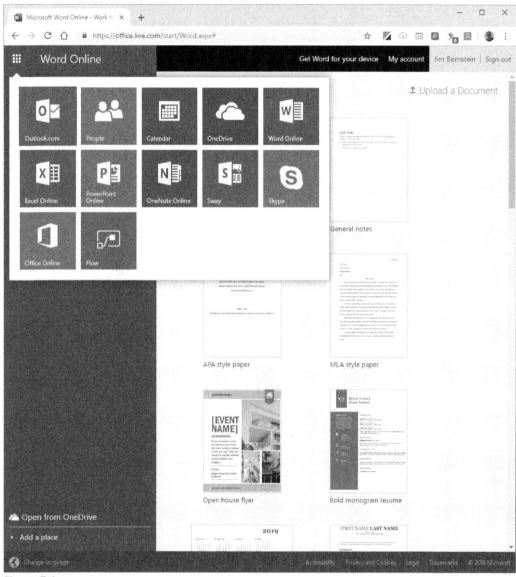

Figure 7.1

For my example, I am going to click on Word Online and open up one of the built-in template documents (as shown in figure 7.2). If you are familiar with the desktop version of Word, you will notice how the ribbon (toolbar) looks very similar to the one you are used to seeing with the regular Word program. You can do things such as change the font, colors, text size, layout, and so on just like in the desktop version. Of course, the desktop version and Office 365 version will have more advanced features, and that's why they are not free!

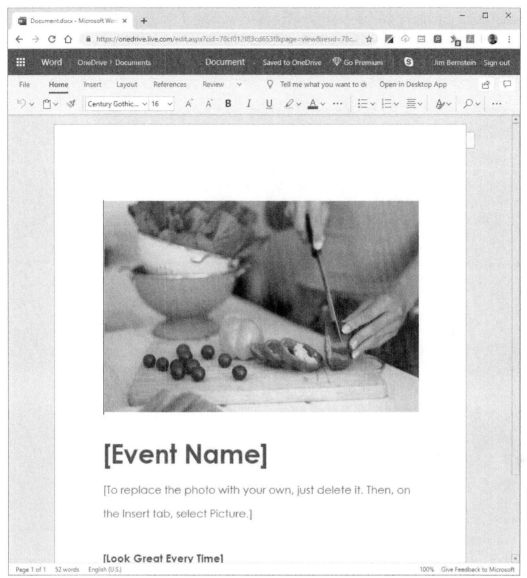

Figure 7.2

By default, Office Online will save your work to your OneDrive online storage account—which you get for free, but if you want to save your work to your computer, then you will need to go to the *Save As* option from the *File* menu, choose *Download a Copy*, and then choose where you want to save the file on your desktop PC.

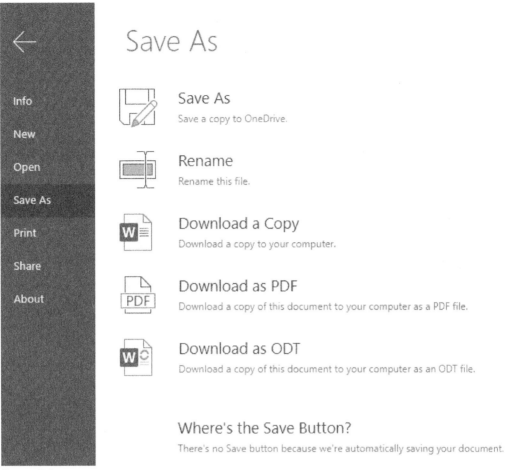

Figure 7.3

One benefit of saving your files to your online storage is that you will have the ability to share them and allow others to collaborate with you without having to email the documents back and forth.

As I mentioned earlier, Google offers a similar service that they call *Google Apps*, and it's free as well unless you want to use the corporate version that they call G Suite, but the free version of their apps should work just fine for you. Figure 7.4 shows the Google Apps menu where you can choose from some of the available applications. There are many more you can use than what is shown here, but in order to get to them, you will have to go to that specific site. For example, if you want to use the Google Calendar then you will need to go to https://calendar.google.com, or just do a search for it and sign in with your Google account.

Once again, I am going to use the Google version of Word (which is called Google Docs) by clicking on it from the available choices. Then I will open one of their built-in template files (figure 7.5).

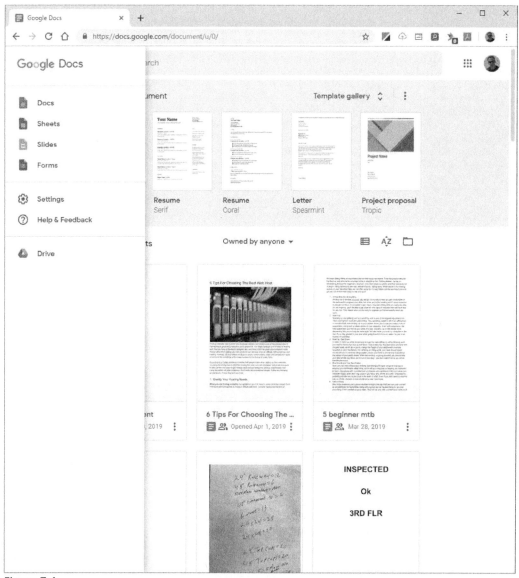

Figure 7.4

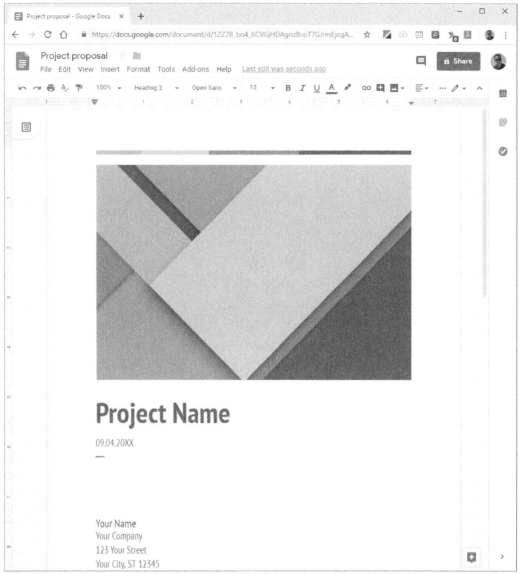

Figure 7.5

As you can see, the interface looks similar to Word Online, and when it comes to saving your files they will go to your Google Drive unless you *specifically* tell Docs to save them to your computer. To do this you will need to go to the *File* menu and then choose *Download as* and pick the format you want to save the file as.

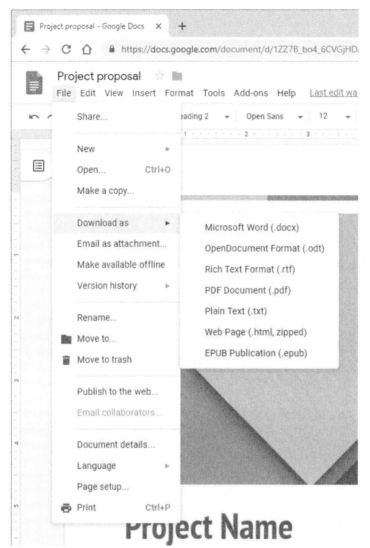

Figure 7.6

I have recently written a book called *Google Apps Made Easy* that contains everything you need to know to get you up and running with all of the most popular applications that Google offers you to use. You can check it out here: https://www.amazon.com/dp/1798114992

Feel free to play around with these services and applications to see if they are something you want to use for yourself in case you feel like expanding your skillset to include "cloud computing", as it's often referred to.

**Online Storage and Backup Services**

I mentioned in the last section how when you use online applications that they prefer that you save your files in their provided online storage repository, which has its pros and cons just like everything else. But you can do much more than just save your documents in this storage, and can actually use it to save other types of files, store backups of your computer, and also share files with others.

Just like with the office-type applications, there are many online storage services you can choose from as well depending on your needs. Most of them offer a free version of the service with limited storage capabilities and features, and then also a pay-for version that is more suited towards business users. If you like, you can have more than one of these accounts at a time to use.

Once again, I will use Microsoft and Google for my examples, even though there are many other options you can use.

I also have a book called *Cloud Storage Made Easy* that contains everything you need to know to get you up and running with all of the most popular, free cloud storage applications. You can check it out here for more details: https://www.amazon.com/dp/1730838359

If you are not the type that backups up their computer, then using one of these cloud storage apps is a good idea because it's free way to get a copy of your important files off of your computer or other device and into a location where they can be recovered in case your computer gets damaged or you lose your smartphone, etc. Many of these apps even come with software you can run on your computer that will synchronize your files within your storage automatically.

The first app I will discuss is from Microsoft, and is called OneDrive. If you are running Windows 10 on your computer at home, then you most likely already have it installed. Figure 7.7 shows my OneDrive folders and files, and you can create new folders as needed to keep your files organized just like you can on your computer. If you take a look at the lower left hand corner, it shows that I have used 130MB out of my free 5GB of storage (1024MB = 1GB). If you need additional storage, then you can sign up for one of the pay-for plans that gives you more room and more features.

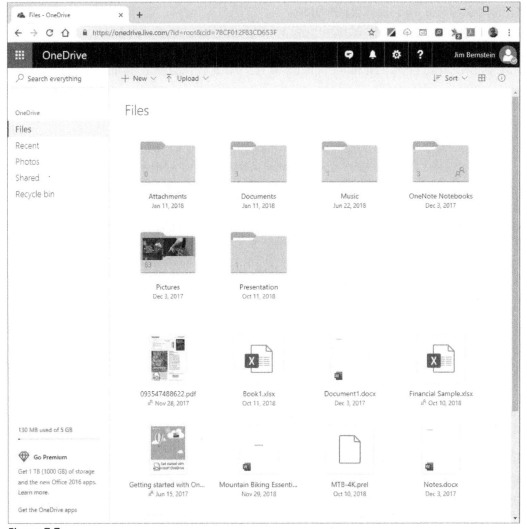

Figure 7.7

If you were to click on one of the files within your OneDrive storage, then it will try to open that file within your browser (if it's possible). Figure 7.8 shows what happens when I click on the *Financial Sample.xlsx* file from figure 7.7. OneDrive was able to open it using Office Online within my web browser.

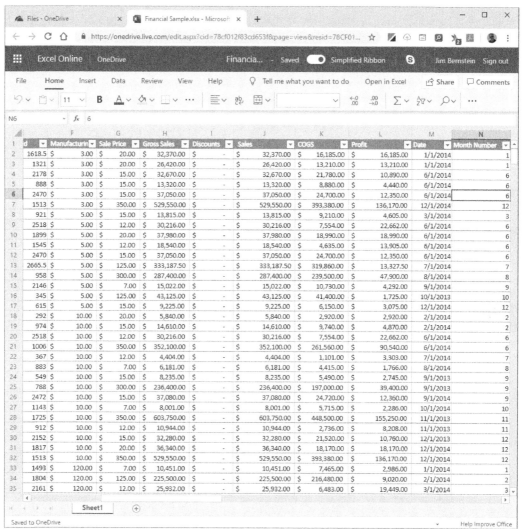

Figure 7.8

When I try to open a file that is not supported to open in a web browser, then I get a message like the one shown in figure 7.9. You will then have the option to download the file to your computer or device and open it from there using one of your installed programs.

MTB-4K.prel

Hmm... looks like this file doesn't have a preview we can show you.

Figure 7.9

Figure 7.10 shows the new options that appear at the top of the page when you select a file. You can see that you have choices such as sharing it with other people, downloading the file to your computer, and even viewing other versions of the file that you have uploaded.

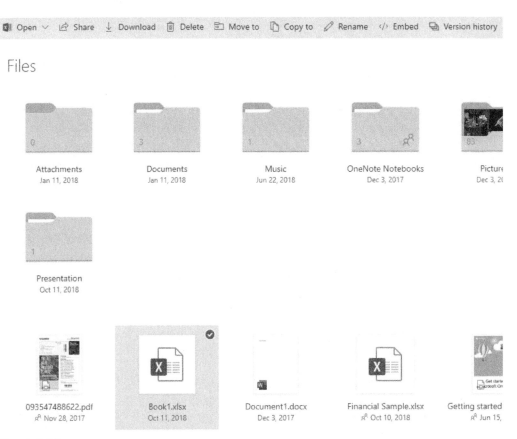

Figure 7.10

Next, I will show you what my Google Drive online storage account looks like. As you can see from the image below, it looks similar to the Microsoft OneDrive interface, and you can actually change the view of the files and folders from a list view (as shown) to more of a thumbnail\preview view (as was seen in my OneDrive example).

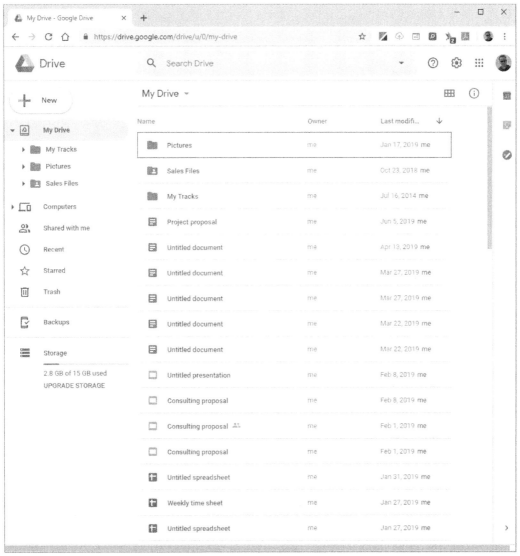

Figure 7.11

If you look closely, you will see that Google gives you 15GB of free storage space compared to the 5GB from Microsoft. And if you need more than that, you can certainly pay to upgrade as well. If you take a look at figure 7.12, you will see a *Backup* section that will show you any backups that you have configured between your computer or devices and your Google Drive storage.

The *Computers* section will show what computers you have synced with your Google Drive and what folders on that computer you have chosen to synchronize.

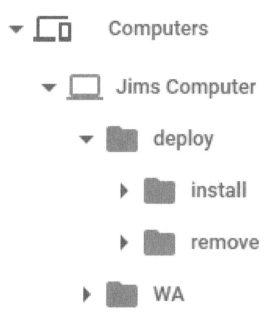

Figure 7.12

There is much more that you can do with these online storage applications, but the goal was just to give you an idea of how they work and let you know they existed just in case you didn't know.

**Online Banking and Bill Paying**
One of my favorite things about the Internet is not having to write checks, address envelopes, and buy stamps to pay my bills. And even better, I like how I don't have to get paper bills in the mail that I end up having to shred because I don't need to keep them for any reason. (Plus, all the unnecessary tree killing!) It's also nice to be able to check your credit card balance and purchases any time you want.

Thanks to online banking and bill paying, it's much easier to stay organized and make sure all your bills are paid on time. The only downside is having to risk exposing your information such as account numbers, your social security number, usernames, and passwords online since it's all going over the Internet to a server who knows where. But if you use caution (and common sense), you will be just fine. Plus, most banks and credit cards offer protection against online theft and fraud.

Once you have an account with your bank or utility company, it's very easy to sign up for an online account. Simply go to their website and enter your information to prove it's you. This information might be in the form of an account number, credit card number, name, address, and so on. (Just make sure you are on the official site for that company before giving out any of this information!)

Then once you have your account configured, you simply sign in with the username and password you created and you are good to go. (Many times your username will be your email address.)

It's a good idea to provide your phone number when signing up for an online account because it can be used to verify it's really you when logging in from a new device, or if you need to reset your password in case you forget it.

Figure 7.13 shows a typical credit card site where you can see things such as the balance owed, credit limit, payment information, payment due date, recent transactions, and more. All of this information is at your fingertips any time you need it, and if you want to see something like an older statement, all you need to do is choose an older date.

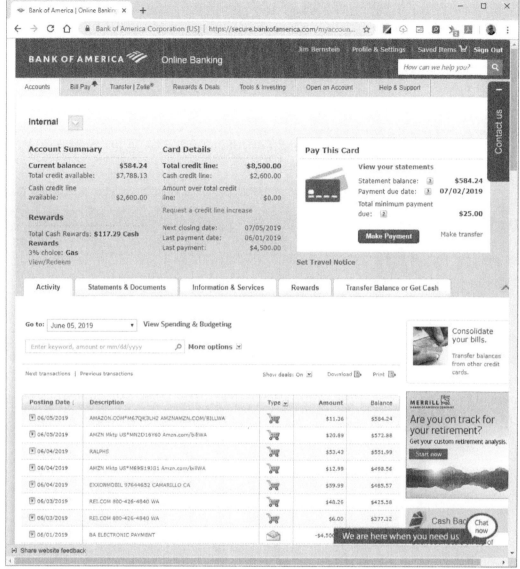

Figure 7.13

To make a payment in this example, you would just click the *Make Payment* button, put in the amount you wish to pay and the date you wish to pay it, and they will take care of the rest. You will need to first set up a payment method such as your checking account beforehand in order for them to have a place to take the money from.

Like I've said many times thought out this book, what you see in my examples will not always look exactly like what you will see when you try this yourself because each website is different, plus the web browser and device you use will make a difference as well. (And yes, I will be saying this again later in the book, so get used to it!)


**Online Games**

The Internet is not just about doing research and paying bills, but also for having fun and killing (or wasting) time. And what better way to kill some time than with video games? When you think about playing video games, you might think that you need a game console like a PlayStation or Xbox, but there are actually many great games you can play on your computer, smartphone, or tablet.

When playing games on a smartphone or tablet you usually need to install the app for that game and then it will connect you to the Internet so you can play along with other people (if it's in fact that type of game). There are also many games that you can play by yourself without needing to interact with others.

For computer games you can also have standalone video games that you install like you would any other software, and then play either by yourself or online with other people. If you go the online route, then you will need to have an Internet connection, of course, and for many of these games it's better to have a faster connection to avoid lag (delays) in your games.

The type of online games I want to discuss don't involve purchasing or installing any software to play and are played via your web browser. **One thing I want to stress is if you find a free online game and it wants you to download and install something to play it, then you should say no and get off that website because it's most likely going to install some type of spyware on your computer that will be used to do things like track your web surfing or steal your personal information**.

Since I'm not a "gamer" I can't tell you which gaming sites are the best, but you can do a search for something like *online games* or *free online games* and see what you come up with. As you can see in figure 7.14, I get a mere 15 billion results when I search for online games, so have fun searching through all of the results!

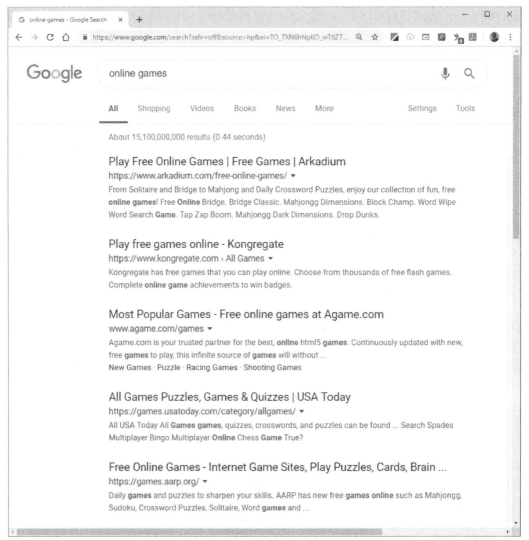

Figure 7.14

Figure 7.15 shows what I get when I click on the first link. As you can see, there are many types of games to choose from, and even a search box where you can search for a particular type of game.

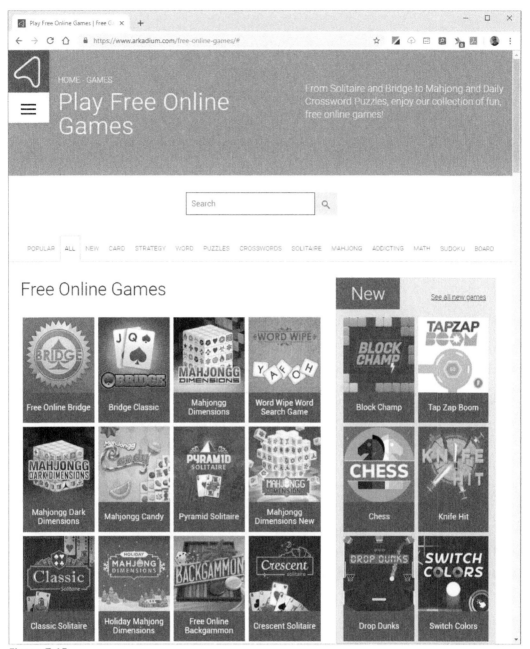

Figure 7.15

Next, I clicked on Classic Solitaire, and then the game loads and I am able to play. Did you notice in figure 7.16 how the screen is filled with advertisements? That is what makes the games free because they are hoping you will click on one of their ads and make some money for them. When you see things like those *Start Now* buttons they are generally trying to make you think you should click on them to play the game, but it's really only an ad.

Figure 7.16

So just remember to be careful when playing free games online. There is usually a catch because, as we all know, nothing is really free!

# Chapter 8 – Social Media

Social media has been a growing part of the online experience for many years now, and if you haven't gotten on the bandwagon, you are missing out (well, that depends on who you talk to!). There are so many social media sites and apps now that it's impossible to cover them all (since some of them disappear as fast as they show up), so I will go over the major players in this chapter.

For the most part, social media is a good way to connect with friends and family that you aren't able to see on a regular basis. It's also a great way to promote something like a business or charity to get more people aware that they exist. (Of course, you also have the people who abuse these sites by promoting illegal and immoral things or by trying to scam others out of money etc.)

**Facebook**
One of the most popular social media sites in the world is Facebook, which has been around since 2004. From what I've heard from the younger generation, it's not "what the kids are into" these days, but it's still very popular among "older" generations. There is a lot that you can do on Facebook, but I will just go over the most common features to get you up and running so you can decide if you want to be a member or not.

Facebook is a way for you to post stories, pictures, movies, website links, and so on for things that you are interested in or are involved in. Many people use it to do things like post pictures of their pets or vacations or complain about their co-workers etc., while others use it to make their followers aware of a certain cause that they are passionate about.

When I say followers, what I mean is the people that are following them on the Facebook site. You can't just follow anyone you want, but have to do what is called a *friend request,* which has to be accepted by the person you have sent the request to. So, if you did a search for Joe Smith and find the Joe Smith you are looking for, you can send him a friend request. Then Joe can either accept or reject that request. If he accepts it, then you will be able to see what Joe is posting on his Facebook page and interact with his posts by doing things such as giving them "likes" and making comments on the posts.

Facebook uses what they call a timeline on your main page that shows you posts from people that you are friends with, and also other people or groups that you follow. For example, if you like the band The Beatles, you can find their Facebook page and then click on Like. You will then be following them and will see their posts in your timeline. For pages like this, you don't need to be accepted in order to see their posts because they are public pages that people (including you) can create in order to get exposure from others. Figure 8.1 shows what I get when searching for The Beatles. The first result is their fan page, which you can follow by clicking on the *Like* button. Then there are some other groups that people have made to discuss The Beatles that you can join if you wish to.

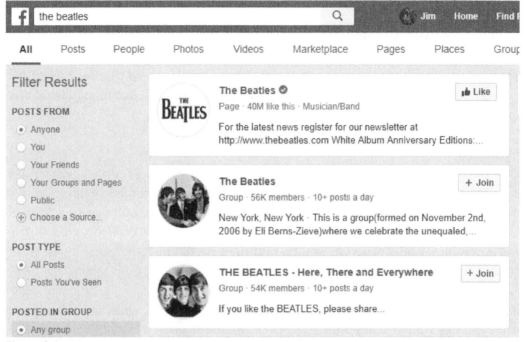

Figure 8.1

Figure 8.2 shows my Facebook home page, and, as you can see, there is a lot going on here, so it's easy to get overwhelmed if you are new to the site. But just because it's there doesn't mean you need to use it. If you just want to use Facebook to keep in touch with friends, then it's pretty easy to use and you can then ignore all the other features if you don't think you will want to use them.

The left hand column shows you all the types of areas that you can go to within Facebook such as finding friends, playing games, checking out movies, and so on. The right side of the page shows which of your friends are either online, or have been online recently. If there is a green dot next to their name, then that means they are currently online (either on their computer or mobile device) and you can send them an instant message if you want to start up a conversation. Instant messages works sort of like the text messages on your phone. If you have created any Facebook pages for things like groups or hobbies, they will show up at the top right. As you can see, I have pages for my mountain bike site and my computer help site.

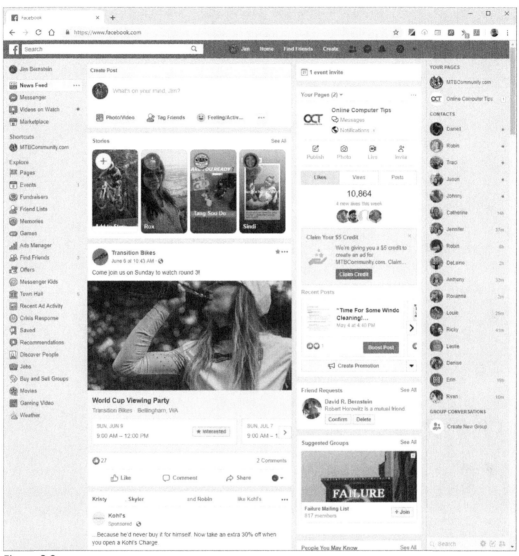

Figure 8.2

The middle of the page shows your feed, which will consist of posts from your friends and also other pages you follow (such as the one in my Beatles example). It will also display advertisements, so don't get confused if something shows up you don't recognize. You will also see things like suggested groups, friend requests, and so on.

At the top of the page there is a Create Post section where you can post anything that is on your mind and also attach things like photos, videos, your location, and so on. You can also decide where you want your post to show and who can see it.

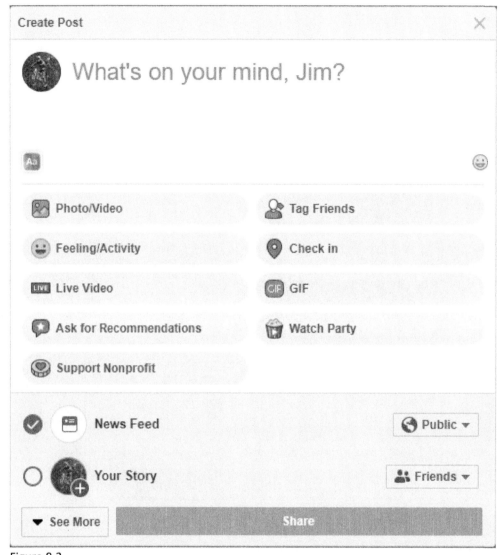

Figure 8.3

Also at the top of the page is a link with your name on it. Clicking on that will show you the posts you have recently made as well as other things such as your bio, friend information, likes, etc.

Speaking of who can see your posts and other information about you, I would take the time to go through some of the Facebook settings to make sure your privacy settings are the way you want them to be so only the people you *want* to see your information can see it.

If you click on the down arrow in the toolbar, you will see the option for Settings (this is also where you will go to logout). Once you are in the Facebook settings, you will see that there are many settings that you can configure, but I will be focusing on the ones that are geared more towards privacy and security.

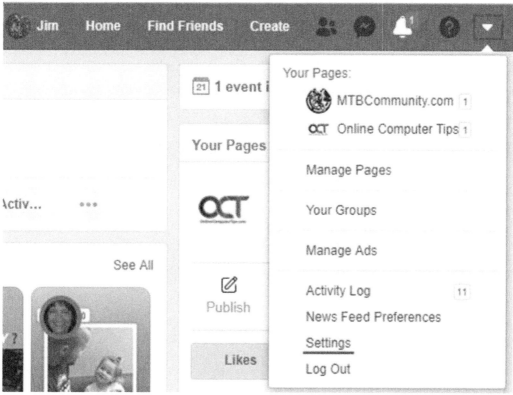

Figure 8.4

The first section I want to discuss is called Security and Login (figure 8.5), and it has settings for things such as how you log into Facebook and extra security options that you can enable.

The section labeled *Recommended* is where you can choose 3 to 5 friends that you trust to help you get back into your account if you forgot your password and have no idea what it could possibly be. What you would do is contact one of these friends, and they can use their Facebook account to contact them about helping you get back on to yours.

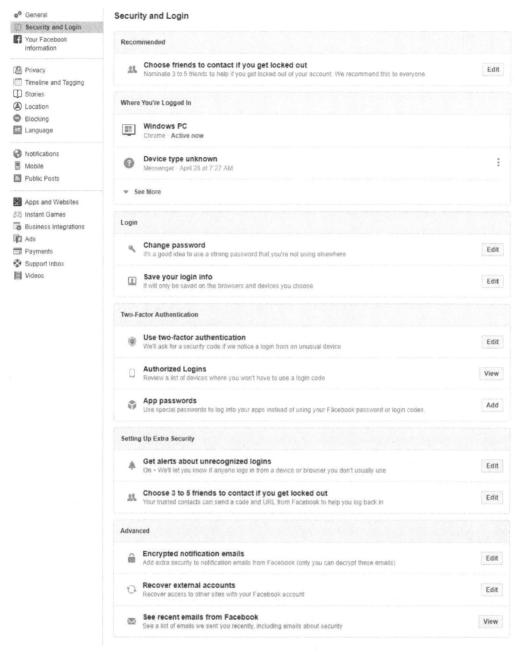

Figure 8.5

Next, we have the *Where You're logged In* section, and this is used to show you where your account is logged in and on what type of device. So, if you think someone is getting into your account, you can go here and look for a location or device that you don't recognize and then take corrective action (such as changing your password).

182

You also have the option to use *Two-Factor Authentication* every time you log into your account to give you extra security against others using your account without your permission. For example, if you log into Facebook on a new device for the first time, it will have you prove it's you by sending a text message to your phone with a verification code.

Next, I would like to go over some of the settings in the *Privacy* section. Here you can tell Facebook who you want to see the posts that you make on your timeline. For example, if you click on *Edit* for the *Who can see your future posts* option, you will get choices similar to figure 8.6, which allows you the ability to fine-tune who can see your activity.

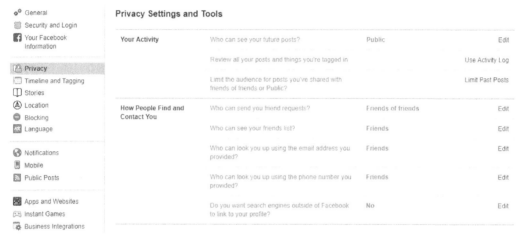

Figure 8.6

Figure 8.7

You can configure settings for similar things such as who can see your friends list, who can see your email address, who can see your phone number, and so on. I would definitely go through this section and adjust any of the options as needed.

Lastly, I would like to discuss the *Timeline and Tagging* section (figure 8.8). This is another privacy setting that you can edit so others don't go posting things about you that you don't want posted. It's not foolproof, but it will help to adjust these settings.

The *Timeline* options can be adjusted so you can decide who can post on your timeline. The options are your friends, or only you. At this time you can't pick and choose which friends can post on your timeline. The *Who can see what others post on your timeline* section *will* let you customize your choices though.

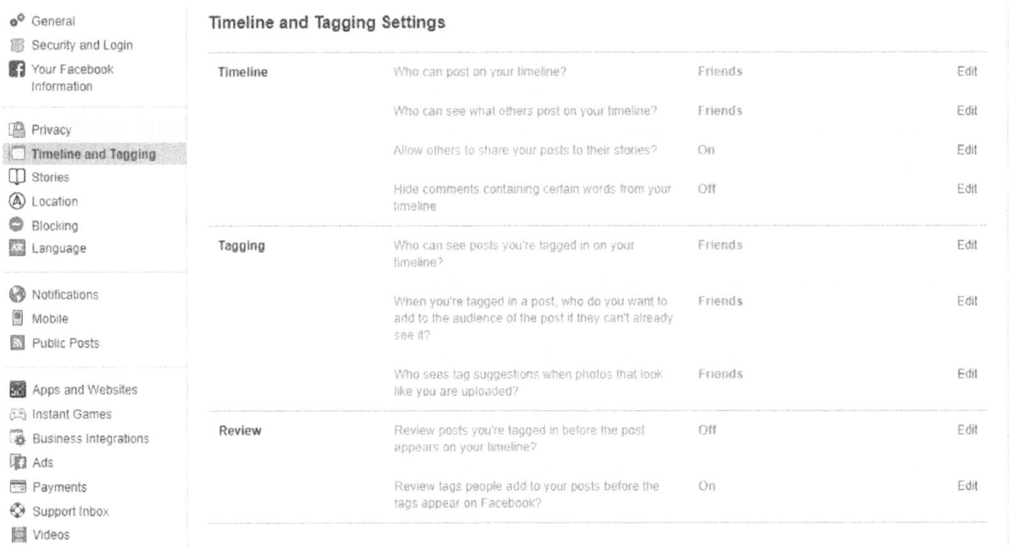

Figure 8.8

*Tagging* is when someone mentions you in one of their posts or adds a picture of you to their post. You can control who can do this with these options. So, if you don't want your name to appear in other people's posts without your permission, you should check out these options for sure.

As you can see from the images above, there are many other settings you can adjust to make Facebook work the way you want it to work. Just keep in mind that no matter how tight you lock things down, Facebook will always have access to your data, and you can't always trust them to do the right thing with it.

**Instagram**

If you are into sharing pictures of things like your pets, vacations, friends, or just about anything else, then Instagram is for you, since that's pretty much what Instagram is used for. You can view yours and other's Instagram accounts on your computer, but if you want to post to Instagram, you will need to do it on a mobile device such as your smartphone or tablet.

When you create an Instagram account you are the only one who will see your posts until you start acquiring followers, and then they will see your posts every time you upload a picture to your feed. So, if you make an account and want others to follow you, then you will need to notify them and tell them to look up your account name on Instagram to start following you.

You can follow others as well, and they don't even need to be people you know. Many people (such as celebrities or athletes) make their accounts public so anyone can follow them. If you don't want your account to be seen by anyone except people you want to see it, then you can make it private. Business accounts won't have this option, but you will most likely be using a personal account anyway. Once you make your account private, people will have to send you a follow request to see your posts, your followers list, or your following list.

Figure 8.9 shows an example of a post from my mountain bike Instagram account when looking at it on a smartphone. It shows how many likes that particular post got, as well as any comments that my followers have left about that post.

Figure 8.9

Followers can click on the heart icon to like the post or click on the speech bubble icon to leave a comment. They can also share my posts with other people via things like email or text message etc.

Figure 8.10 shows how my account looks on a web browser when using a personal computer. Notice how you can still do the same things such as like and comment on posts.

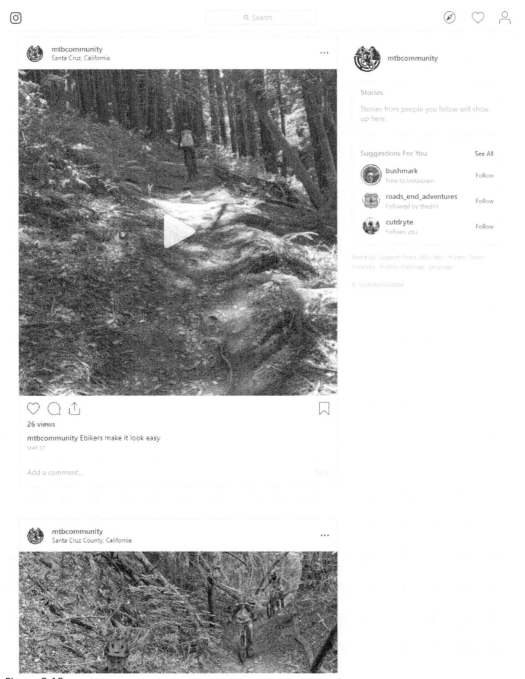

Figure 8.10

To create an account all you need to do is install the Instagram app on your device if it's not there already. Then sign up with a username, email address, and password. Since there are so many Instagram accounts already active, it might take you a bit to find a name that is not already in use.

Then all you need to do is click on the + button (which can be seen at the bottom of figure 8.9) and you will be asked where you want to get your photo (or video) from that you wish to post. You can choose from pictures you already have on your device, or you can take one on the spot to post.

Next, you will have the option to enhance your picture with a filter to change the way it looks (figure 8.11).

Figure 8.11

Then you can add some text describing the picture. In my example I added *Fun times on the mountain*. Then you can add what they call a tag to your post. Tags are used to reference other people, companies, products, websites, and so on. You create a tag by adding the pound or hash sign (#) to the front of the word you are using for your tag. These are also referred to as hashtags. As you start typing in your hashtag (starting with the # symbol), Instagram will give you suggestions based on what you are typing. You can choose the one that matches, or add your own if they don't have a suggestion for you (figure 8.12).

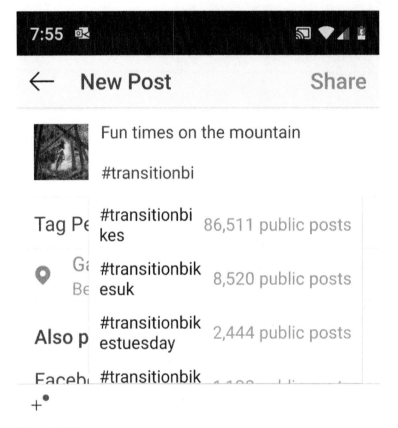

Figure 8.12

You can also add a location to your post so people know where the picture was taken. Instagram will give you suggestions based on your location by using the GPS on your phone. You can also manually type in a location. If your Instagram account is linked to your Facebook, Twitter, or Tumblr account, then you can have your picture automatically posted there as well.

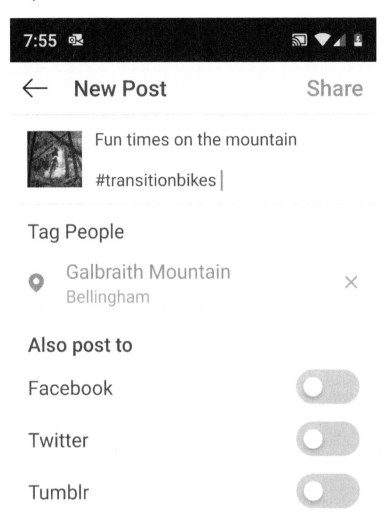

Figure 8.13

Once everything looks good, you will click on Share, and then your picture will be posted and show up in all of your follower's feeds on their accounts.

**Twitter**

Twitter is similar to Instagram except it's used more for posting comments or opinions rather than pictures (even though you can add those as well). You can use your mobile devices and computer to post to your Twitter account, as well as read other people's posts (which are called *Tweets*).

Just like with Facebook and Instagram, all you need to do is sign up for a free account and you will be ready to start posing. But, once again, you will need to get yourself some followers if you want anyone to read about what you have to say.

Figure 8.14 shows my computer support site Twitter account. On the top you can see that I have made 851 tweets to my 196 followers. Then you can see my latest post was about the release of my previous book called Windows Home Networking Made Easy.

Figure 8.14

To create a new post, all I need to do is click on the Tweet button on the top right of the page and fill in the details about my tweet (figure 8.15). In my example I am going to share a website link about an upcoming Gmail update. I am also going to include the Gmail icon image to enhance my post and make it stand out more. As of now, you can have a maximum of 280 characters per post. (By characters I mean letters, numbers, special characters, and so on.) When you add a website address like I did, it will count towards the character limit.

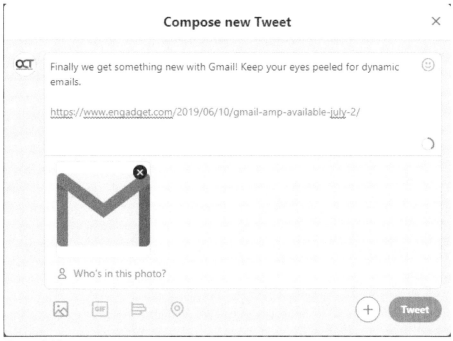

Figure 8.15

I then clicked on the *add image* button on the bottom left of the box and added the Gmail logo picture that I had saved on my computer. You can add other items such as a poll, location, and even emoji characters. When you are ready to add your witty and profound comment, simply click on the *Tweet* button and it will be posted to your account and your followers will see it as well. Figure 8.16 shows my account after adding my new Tweet.

Figure 8.16

# Chapter 9 – Staying Safe and Secure Online

If you are new to the Internet, or just not a very tech-savvy person, then this will be one of the most important chapters for you to focus on because the Internet can be a dangerous place and it seems to be getting worse and worse every year. There are many websites out there that will try and get you to give them your personal information, buy services you will never get, or ones that will even install software on your computer to take advantage of you without you even knowing it. Plus, you still need to worry about these types of things happening with email that you most likely get on a regular basis.

There is a lot to cover in this chapter, so it will be one of the longer ones, but like I just said, it's one of the most important ones to read in order to stay as safe as you can while online. I will be going over a variety of topics to cover all of the areas you need to be careful in while connected to the Internet.

**Common Types of Online Threats**
There are many ways for people to get to you online, and in this section I will go over the most commonly used methods these "cybercriminals", as they are often called, use to commit their crimes.

The first one I want to discuss is what is known as a *drive by attack* or *drive by download*. This is when you go to a website and some type of software or file gets downloaded to your computer that is used to do things such as steal your personal information or cause unwanted popup ads, etc. This term can also be used when you purposely download software from a website thinking it's one thing, but it turns out to be something malicious.

Unfortunately, many of these sites are good at tricking the those who are too trusting or may not know any better, and once you go to that site it's too late and then you will need to find a way to clean this "malware infection", as it is called, from your computer. Many times this software is very good at keeping itself hidden so you don't even know it's there. I will be discussing security software later in this chapter, but many of these products can actually tell when this process is happening and block it or prevent you from going to the malicious site at all.

What you can do on your end is not go to any type of website that you don't think is legitimate. Many times people will get this type of malware (or spyware as it's also called) infection when looking for things like free music or movie downloads. These cybercriminals will prey on those looking to get something for free that would normally not be free. Pornography sites are also notorious for spreading malware so stay of those if you can as well.

Another scam you may come across is getting a message on your computer saying that you have some type of virus or spyware infection and you need to call a certain number to get it fixed otherwise your computer will stop working and you may even lose your personal files. Many times these messages will say they are from Microsoft trying to legitimize themselves. Then once you call the number they will ask for your credit card first, and then have you help them get on your computer remotely so they can "fix" the problem that was not even there to begin with. Figure 9.1 shows an example of what this message can look like, but they can vary dramatically in their appearance.

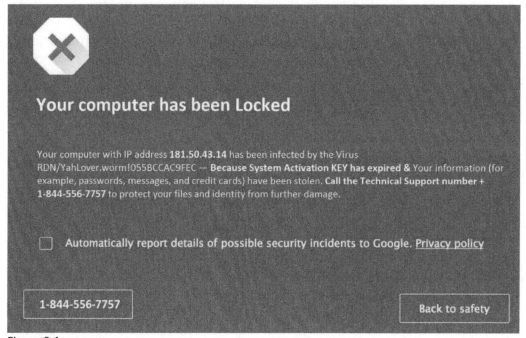

Figure 9.1

Many times they will often install malware on your computer while pretending to fix it, so it's a double whammy because you lost money and also made your computer worse off than it was before. Just remember that Microsoft, Apple, Dell, HP, and so on will *never* call you to tell you that your computer has malicious software installed on it (they have better things to do!).

If this happens to you, just try and close out the message and your web browser, and if that doesn't work then shut down your computer. If you are prevented from that, then you will need to hold down the power button to force the power off or pull the plug from the wall and hope everything works correctly after you turn your computer back on.

 It's never a good idea to simply turn off your computer without properly shutting it down because you risk file corruption and data loss that may make your computer not want to start back up again. This applies to computers running Windows as well as Macs.

Another common way for cybercriminals to get your personal information is to create fake websites that copy legitimate websites in order to trick you into giving up your personal information such as passwords, credit card numbers, social security numbers, and so on.

They do this by duplicating an existing website, and many of them look so much like the real website that it's hard to tell the difference unless you know what you are looking for. Some things that will give away the fraudulent sites are spelling and grammar errors as well as low quality graphics and odd looking text.

The way to distinguish the real site from the fake site is by its URL, or address. Many times these sites will have a similar address, but just be off by one letter hoping you won't be looking or notice the difference. For example, if your banking site address is **http://www.safebank.com,** then they might make a fake site with an address of **http://saferbank.com** and count on you not noticing the difference. Then they would send you a fake or spoofed email with a link to the fake site saying something like there is a problem with your account and hope that you go there and log in, which will give them your name and password to the real site that they can use for their own evil purposes. Thankfully you can't have two websites with the exact same address, otherwise we would all be in a load of trouble!

There are other types of online threats you should be aware of as well, and I will be covering more of them in detail in the following sections.

**Secure vs. Unsecure Websites**
By now you should have realized that the Internet is not a 100% safe place to be and that there are risks involved when going online. Thankfully there are some methods that are used to help keep you safe when surfing the Internet. One of these methods involves securing websites in order to assure you that you are

going to the site you want to be going to. To make a website secure, the administrator needs to purchase a certificate from a trusted certificate authority and install in on the website to prove that they are who they say they are, and that all information passed back and forth between your computer or device and the website is over a secure connection. Most modern web browsers will let you know when your connection is secure or unsecure, but still let you access the site either way.

Just because a website is not secure doesn't mean that it can't be trusted and that you should avoid going to it. Many websites don't have any need to be secured because they are just for informational purposes and there is no need for you to input any personal information while on that site.

You might have noticed that website addresses begin with http even though many browsers hide the http and even the www in the address bar. When a site begins with http, that means it's not secure, and your browser should display a warning like the one seen in figure 9.2 (which is actually my mountain bike website).

Figure 9.2

On my computer website, I do have a certificate installed, and many websites are going with certificates even if they really don't need them just so they can assure you of their security. Notice in figure 9.3 that the address begins with https, and the S at the end stands for secure. There is also a lock icon next to the address indicating that it's a secure website.

Figure 9.3

Not all web browsers will show secure and unsecure websites the same, but it should be easy to figure out if the site is secure or not. For example, figures 9.4 and 9.5 show two other browsers, and you can see how they both use the same lock icon to indicate a secure website.

Figure 9.4

Figure 9.5

If you are going to a website where you will be logging in with a username and password or entering any kind of personal information into a form, then you need to make sure that it is a secure website, otherwise you risk getting your information stolen. If it's a banking website or shopping website, then you *really* need to make sure that it is secure otherwise you are asking for trouble. Any banking or shopping website that is not secure should not be up and running, and might even be a fake site to begin with.

**Email Safety**

If you are an active Internet user, then you most likely have an email account as well that you use for personal or business emails. I'm sure from time to time (or daily) you have received emails from people that you don't know or about subjects that don't concern you at all.

Just like they do with websites, cybercriminals will try and get to you via your email as well, so always be careful when opening any email you get, even if it's from someone you know. There are many ways these individuals will try and trick you in order to get your personal data or infect your computer with some sort of malware.

*Spoofed Emails*

The first email safety topic I want to discuss involves spoofing emails with names and addresses you know in order to trick you into thinking it's from someone you trust when, in fact, it's not. Spoofing an email involves either putting in the name of someone you know as the sender, or having their real email address displayed, or maybe even both.

When you create an email account, you can put in whatever name you like for the display name, which is what is shown to the person you send an email to. So, if someone knows the name of someone you trust, then it's easy to just put that name as their display name and hope you don't check the email address to make sure it's really them.

It's also possible for an actual email address to be spoofed so it looks like it's really coming from that person. If you are not careful, then you can be tricked by this as well. There are ways to check the real email address of a sender, but that varies depending on what site or program you use to access your email. You might have even received an email from yourself at one time and wonder how that was possible, and that's a perfect example of address spoofing.

*Fake Website Links*
Another common practice is to add a fake website link in the body of an email hoping you click on it so it will take you to maybe a fake version of that website or another site where it installs some malware on your computer without you knowing it.

It's easy to have the link display text be different from where the website is actually taking you, so you should always confirm where it's going. Most of the time you can hover your mouse over the link and it will tell you the real address of the website (as seen in figure 9.6). As you can see, the display text for the link shows **www.safebank.com** while the real address is actually **www.fakebank.com**. This procedure will be harder or not possible on mobile devices, so you should be extra careful.

http://www.fakebank.com/
Ctrl+Click to follow link

# http://www.safebank.com

Figure 9.6

*Malicious Attachments*
Another thing to watch out for when it comes to email is making sure not to open any attachments that you shouldn't be opening. I know it's hard to tell just by looking at an attachment whether it's safe or not to open, but there are a few things to watch out for to increase your chances of staying safe.

The first rule in opening email attachments **is NEVER OPEN AN ATTACHMENT FROM SOMEONE YOU DON'T KNOW**. This is a very common practice used by cybercriminals to get their way into your computer.

There are several types of attachments you should never open regardless of who they are from. Even if it's from someone you know, there is a good chance their email account got hacked, or someone is spoofing their email address and sending you a malicious attachment. Files generally have what they call file extensions on them, and these file extensions tell your computer or device what program to use to open the file with. For example, a Microsoft Word document will have a .doc or .docx file extension on it telling your computer to open a file called **resume.docx** with Microsoft Word.

Many operating systems, such as Windows, will hide these file extensions by default, so the file I just mentioned will show only as **resume** without the .docx. There is a way to have Windows show the file extensions, but that is beyond the scope of this book, so if you are feeling geeky you can research it yourself and figure out how to get it done (it's not that hard).

Now that I got file extensions out of the way, back to the types of files you *shouldn't* open. There are many dangerous file types that you would never need to open on your computer or device, so if you see any files that end with any of these, just delete the email and remove it from your trash.

- .js
- .exe
- .bat
- .vbs
- .vb
- .dll
- .jar
- .sfx
- .tmp
- .py
- .pif
- .ps

These are not the only files to watch out for, but are some of the more commonly used files that are used to spread malware. Keep in mind that these types of files have legitimate uses on computers, but *not* as email attachments.

There are other types of files that are commonly sent as attachments that can still be malicious, so you still need to be careful even when opening these types of files. Some common examples include:

- **.zip** – Used to compress files to make them smaller.
- **.pdf** – Used by Adobe Acrobat\Reader for documents.
- **.msi** – Used by Windows to install software (not too commonly attached to emails).
- **.docm** – A Microsoft Word file with macros.
- **.xlsm** - A Microsoft Excel file with macros.

This is where having security software installed on your computer will help protect you before it's too late by scanning the file before you even get a chance to open it. (I will be discussing this type of software later in the chapter.)


**Checking URLs\Addresses**
Earlier in this chapter, I discussed secure and unsecure websites but wanted to mention how you should check the website addresses of the sites you go to whenever possible to make sure you are going where you want to go.

If you get to your commonly accessed websites from your bookmarks, then you should be okay because they don't change unless you manually change them. (Just be sure your bookmark addresses are correct to begin with!) But if you do a search for a website such as your banking site, then make sure the link you are clicking on from the search results is the right one.

Figure 9.7 shows the results I get when searching for *Peoples Bank*. As you can see, there are several results, and they all have different addresses, so it's important to know the right address of the site you are trying to go to when it has to do with security, or a site where you might have to enter your personal information.

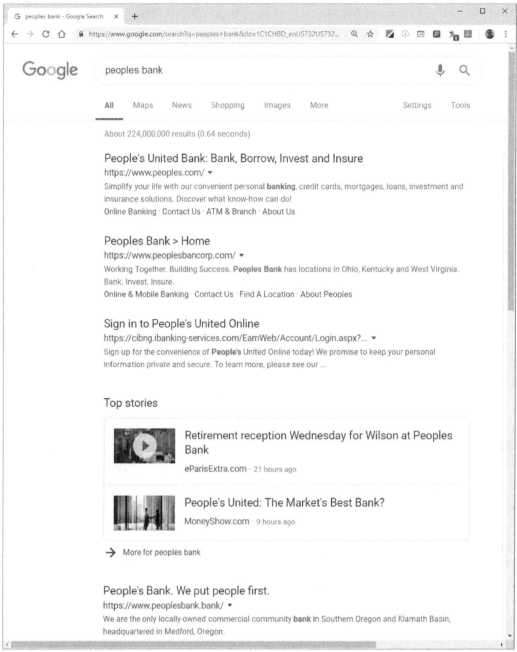

Figure 9.7

If you look closely at all the search results in figure 9.7, you will see that all the addresses start with https, meaning they are secure websites, which is critical for banking sites to be. Try and get in the habit of noticing this in your search results for your own safety.

This also applies when people email or text website addresses to you. Before you click or tap on the link, give it a once over to make sure that everything looks okay so you can have an idea of what website it will be taking you to rather than just blindly clicking and hoping for the best.

**Providing Personal Information**

When you do things like shop or bank online, you are expected to provide certain types of information such as your address, phone number, account number, and so on. But this doesn't mean you should just give any site the information they ask for. If you are on a site that does not require you to give out any information, then there is really no reason to do so. For example, you might go to a website and it will give you a popup to sign up for its mailing list. If you don't plan on using this site again or want to get emails from them, then don't feel obligated to provide them with your email address.

Many times you will go to a website such as a shopping site and it will want to know your location to show you their local stores, or maybe estimate shipping costs. When this happens you may get a popup similar to what is shown in figure 9.8.

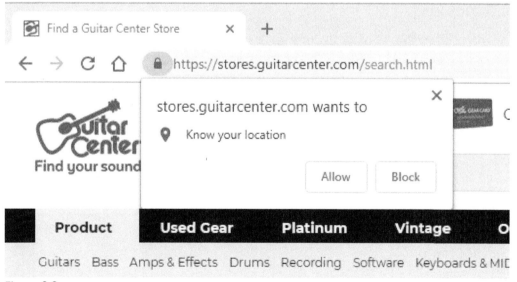

Figure 9.8

If you are okay with providing the site with your location, then you can click on *Allow* and it will tailor its results based on where you are. For the most part, there is no harm in doing this, but if you really don't have a need to give them your location, you might as well click on *Block*.

When shopping online you will often get asked if you want to save information such as your shipping address or credit card number. This is completely up to you because that way you won't need to type in the information each time you buy something from that site. I'm usually okay with saving my address on sites that I use often, but for the most part I don't let them keep my credit card information. (I do make one exception for Amazon.com because of how often I use their site.)

You should **never** give out your social security number unless you are absolutely sure the site is secure and it's actually a site that requires it. When typing it in you should see that what you are typing is hidden as you type. If it's not, then that might be an indication that you shouldn't be entering it in there.

*Saving Your Login Information*

Since technology has made our lives easier, it has unfortunately made us lazier as well. Nobody likes to type in their username and password every time they go to a website or have to remember what password they even use for that site. All web browsers offer the ability to remember login information for specific websites so that when you go to that website, the information is already filled in for you or, better yet, it just logs you in automatically.

For many sites this is okay as long as it's a website that won't cause you any personal or financial problems if someone was to get your login information. But for things such as banking, tax, or medical websites, you should *never* let your web browser save your login information because if someone gets into your computer, they will be able to get your saved names and passwords and will be able to use them to log into things such as your bank accounts, etc.

Figure 9.9 shows some of the saved passwords kept in the Google Chrome web browser. All you need to know to view any of these passwords is the password for the computer itself, so you can see how easy it would be to have all of your usernames and passwords compromised.

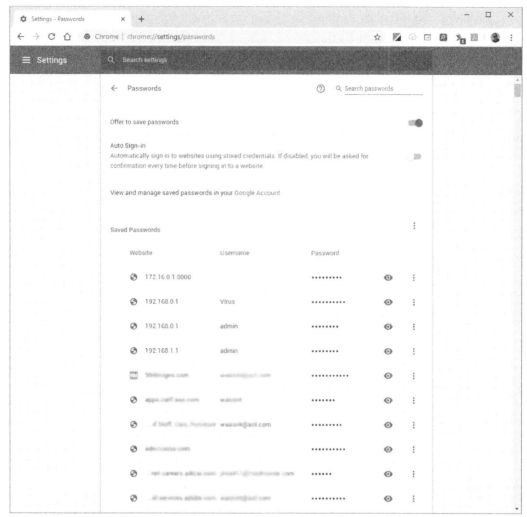

Figure 9.9

If you look closely, you can see the options to turn off the offer to save passwords feature, and also the automatic sign in feature. These settings will vary from browser to browser and device to device.

If you have a saved login that you want to get rid of, you should be able to just remove the saved information for that site rather than have to remove all of them or disable the ability for your web browser to save logins\passwords altogether. (How you do this will vary on your browser and device, of course.)


**Private Browsing**

With online privacy becoming more of a concern lately, there is a growing need to find ways to keep what we are doing online to ourselves. If you use social media, or even have a smartphone, you are giving up more information about what you do and where you go that you might realize, and for many people this is not acceptable.

Since there is a growing desire for privacy, many companies are taking advantage of this need and coming up with ways to keep your web activity more private. One way to do this is to use what is called *private browsing* or *incognito mode* within your web browser, which helps to accomplish this.

The way private browsing works will vary between web browsers, but essentially it makes it so your browser won't keep track of the pages you visit, the data you enter into forms, or any searches you submit. It won't remember what files you download, but those files will stay on your computer after you close your browser, so they will have to be manually deleted if you want them gone. Firefox offers an additional feature called tracking protection which attempts to prevent sites from gathering data about your browsing habits.

Private browsing is not *completely* private, and you should think of it only as protection from others who might use your computer and try to see where you have been. Other apps or programs that track where you go will still be able to see where you are going, as well as your Internet provider since your web traffic has to go through them regardless of whether it's private or not on your end. And if you are at work and they monitor Internet traffic, then private browsing most likely will not hide your activity from your network administrators and their monitoring devices.

The method to use private browsing will vary depending on what web browser you are using. For example, with Google Chrome you will go to the three vertical dots in the upper right hand corner and choose *New incognito window*.

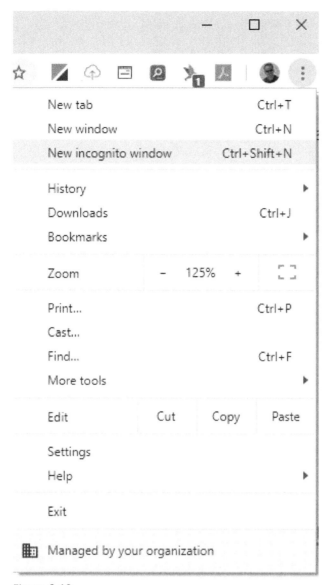

Figure 9.10

For Microsoft Edge you need to go to the three horizontal dots at the top right and choose *New InPrivate window*. For Firefox, go the File menu and choose *New Private Window*. For the Safari browser on your Mac, you would also go to File and then *New Private Window* (figure 9.11). For an iPhone, iPad, or iPod, open Safari, tap the double box icon, and then tap on *Private* and then on *Done*.

Figure 9.11

To exit out of private browsing simply close your browser. The next time you open it, you will be in regular browsing mode.

**Clearing Browser History**

There may come a time when you want to erase where you have been from your browser while in normal browsing mode. This is where clearing your history comes into play, and it's something you can easily do whenever you like. As you access websites, your computer or mobile device keeps track of where you have been and also does things like keeps images from sites so when you go back to that site it doesn't have to re-download the images from that page and rather just loads the ones on your computer, making that site load faster.

Over time your computer can get cluttered with these images and also other temporary files like cookies that your web browser keeps as you visit websites throughout the day. These files take up space on your hard drive, and over time can even slow things down a little, so clearing your history and temporary files is something you might want to think about doing.

Most browsers will let you choose what type of information and files you can delete and also from what time period. So, let's say you want to remove your browsing history for the past week, but leave the rest. You most likely will have an option to do that. Or let's say you want to delete temporary Internet files but keep your cookies. That should be an option you have as well.

Just like with everything else, how you clear your history will vary depending on what web browser you are using, and once again I will be using Google Chrome for my example. (If you need a refresher on history, then go back to Chapter 3 and read the section on it.) To access your history in Chrome simply go to the three vertical dots at the top right and choose *History*.

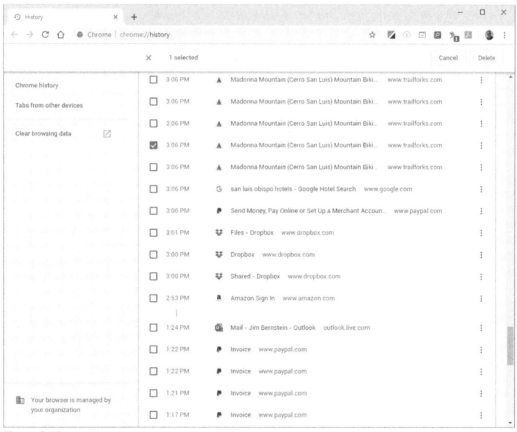

Figure 9.12

Figure 9.12 shows the current history, and you can scroll up and down the list to see where you (or others) have been. If you want to go the webpage related to a specific history item, all you need to do is click on it. Or, if you want to remove a specific history item, simply check the box next to it and click on the *Delete* button.

If I want to remove my history items in bulk, I can click on *Clear browsing history* and I will see a screen similar to figure 9.13. As you can see, I can choose the time range such as all time, the last hour, the last 7 days, and so on. Then I can choose which history items I want to have removed. Normally you can stick with the defaults and be okay, but if you are planning on really clearing out your browser, you can also have any saved passwords and form information (such as saved addresses) removed as well. If you do clear out your saved passwords and form information, you will manually need to enter the info in next time you go to any websites that you had the information stored for previously.

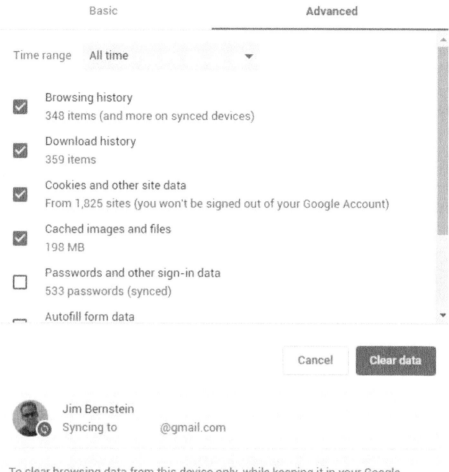

Figure 9.13

Take a look at the bottom of figure 9.13 and you will see that I am syncing my browser information across all my devices that use Google Chrome. That way things like my bookmarks, saved passwords, and history will sync to any device I am logged into my Google account with.

**Popups and Toolbars**

I have mentioned how it's possible that by simply going to a website you can end up with unwanted software installed on your computer and not even know it's happened. But if all of a sudden you are getting lots of pop-up ads while browsing the Internet or have strange toolbars show up in your browser, then that will confirm that you have been a victim of this type of unwanted software installation.

### Popup Ads

Popup ads are exactly what they sound like: ads that pop up out of nowhere on top of whatever webpage you happen to be on. For the most part, you can just close them out, but many times they will just come back over and over and get really annoying. Other times they won't have a way to close them without closing your web browser altogether.

Many websites have legitimate popup ads that might ask you to sign up for their mailing list, ask you to take a survey, offer you a coupon, etc., and this is perfectly normal. Figure 9.14 shows an example of one of these types of popup ads.

Figure 9.14

When you see popups that are telling you that your computer is infected with a virus or that you need some sort of software update to continue, then it's most likely a popup caused by either malware installed on your computer, or from a website that is trying to get you to install or do something you shouldn't be doing. Figures 9.15 and 9.16 show examples of these types of popups.

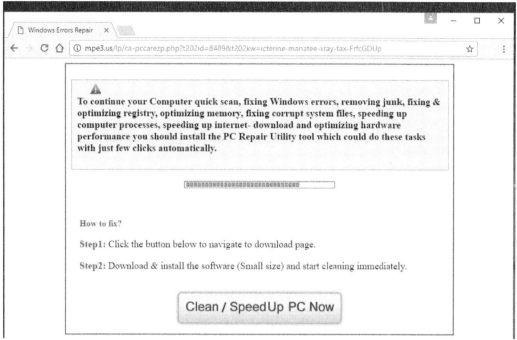

Figure 9.15

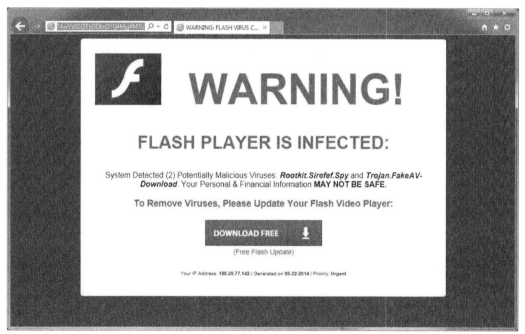

Figure 9.16

The hardest part about dealing with popups is determining which are legitimate and which are caused by malicious software installed on your computer. One way to tell is if you get constant pop-up ads on any website you go to compared to if it's just on a particular site. If it's just on the one site and it doesn't happen when you leave that site and go to another, then it's most likely just the way that website has been designed, and it might be one you want to stay away from. If you get popup ads all the time on any site you go to, then it's probably time to get some antispyware software installed on your computer to see if it can get rid of it. (I will be discussing this type of software later in this chapter.)

*Browser Toolbars*
Browser toolbars are another one of those things that can be legitimate, or caused by malicious software getting installed on your computer. Toolbars are addons to browsers that add additional functionality such as buttons to easily check your email, the weather, or do specific types of searches. Not all toolbars are bad, and some people actually install them on purpose.

Figure 9.17 shows some examples of toolbars that can get installed within your web browser. Many times when this happens you will notice that your homepage also gets changed to match the toolbar that got installed. For example, let's say your homepage was Bing.com and all of a sudden you noticed you had a toolbar called *Social Search* and now your homepage was changed to *Social Search* as well. (FYI, your homepage is the website that loads when you first open your web browser and also what gets loaded when you click the home button in your browser.)

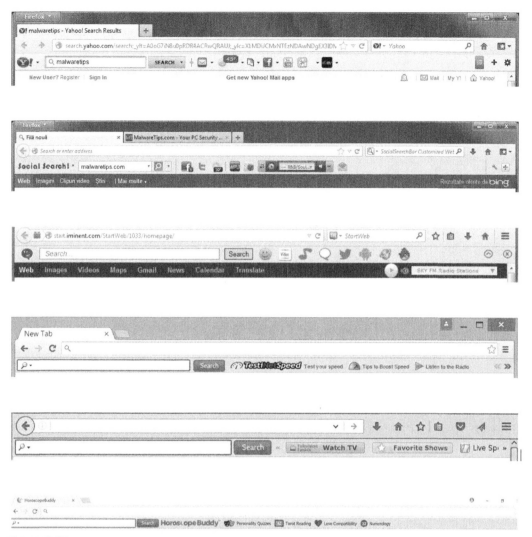

Figure 9.17

Many times all you need to do to get rid of these toolbars is uninstall them from your computer the same way you would uninstall any other type of software. (You may also have to use antispyware software to get rid of them if that doesn't work.) You might also be able to remove them from your browser addons, which I will be discussing next. These toolbars are more of an issue for computers rather than mobile devices, so you don't need to really worry about them in that situation.

*Browser addons\plugins*
Web browsers have the ability to be enhanced by additional software called addons, plugins, or even extensions, which enable extra functionality or features for your browser. You can check to see what addons are installed in your browser and also disable or remove them if you don't want them to be in use or if they

look like they shouldn't be there to begin with. Figure 9.18 shows what extensions are loaded in my Google Chrome browser while figure 9.19 shows what plugins are loaded in my Mozilla Firefox browser. For the most part, you will have some sort of addons installed in your browsers at all times, so don't be alarmed if you do see some there.

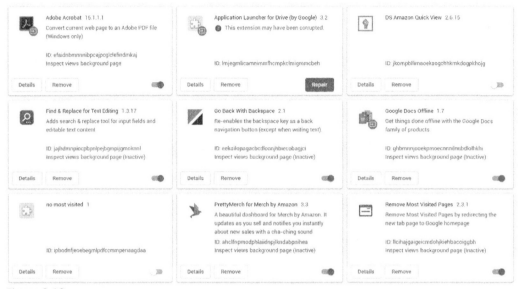

Figure 9.18

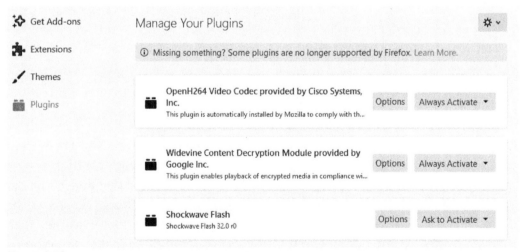

Figure 9.19

Most browsers will allow you to install additional addons for things such as popup blockers, shopping, password managers, music players, and so on. Figure 9.20 shows some of the addons you can install for Firefox, figure 9.21 shows some available extensions for Edge, and figure 9.20 shows some available extensions for Safari.

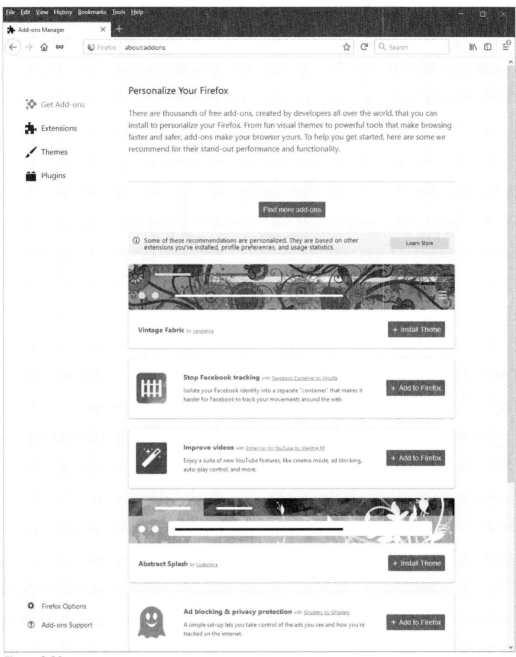

Figure 9.20

# Extensions for Microsoft Edge

Showing 1 - 90 of 270 results

**Amazon Assistant**
★★★☆☆ 929

Free

**Turn Off the Lights for Microsoft Edge**
★★★★☆ 1K

Free

**Save to Pocket**
★★★★☆ 633

Free

**Adblock Plus (Beta)**
★★★☆☆ 6K

Free

**Google Scholar Button**
★★★★☆ 76

Free

**uBlock Origin**
★★★★☆ 3K

Free

**Mailtrack for Gmail & Inbox: Email**
★★★☆☆ 126

Free

**OneNote Web Clipper**
★★★☆☆ 1K

Free

**360 Viewer**
★★★★☆ 483

Free

**AdBlock**
★★★☆☆ 6K

Free

**Translator for Microsoft Edge**

**Tampermonkey**
★★★★☆ 1K

**Night Eye**
★★★☆☆ 184

**360 Internet Protection**

**Boomerang for Gmail**

Figure 9.21

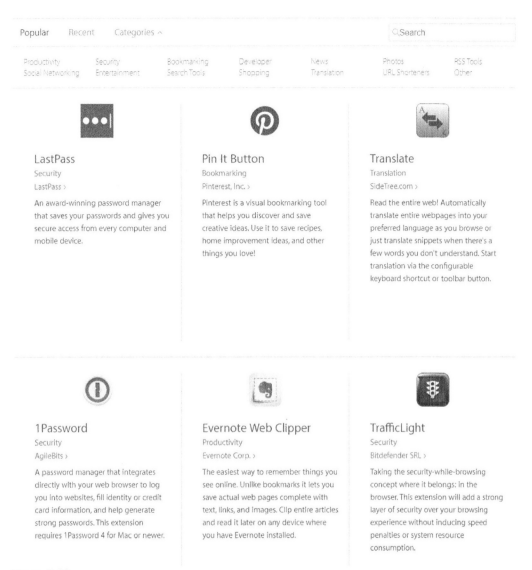

Figure 9.22

When searching for and installing any addons or extensions, it's best to do so from the browser settings or from the browser maker's website itself rather than trusting some type of addon that you might come across on some random site.

### Downloading Files and Software

You might remember that I had an entire chapter on downloading files and software (Chapter 4), but I wanted to take the time to discuss what can happen if you download the wrong types of files and software.

You should know by now that the Internet can be a dangerous place, and there *are* some shady characters out there looking to take advantage of you, so you really need to be careful when it comes to watching what you download online. If you keep your downloading limited to well known, trusted websites, then you should be okay.

For the most part, files like pictures and music should be okay because you can't really do anything to make these types of files dangerous. But let's say you are looking for an instruction manual for your new iPad. This type of document will most likely be in a PDF file format, which is very common and usually safe. But it's possible to create a PDF file that can infect your computer when it's opened. So, if you go to the official Apple website to get this manual, you should be safe, but if you see it listed on a website that doesn't appear too professional or trustworthy, you might want to think twice about downloading it from there. Over time it gets a little easier to tell the good from the bad websites, but it can still be difficult if you are not a techy-type person.

Many sites offer documentation in Microsoft Word format as well, which is also generally safe, but you need to be careful when downloading Word files, too. The same thing goes for zip files, which are also very common. I mentioned potentially dangerous email attachments earlier in this chapter, and those same types of files apply when it comes to downloading files from the Internet.

One thing that you can download that is potentially more dangerous than files is software. In order to install new software on your computer, you need a way to get it there first. This can be done via methods such as CDs, flash drives, and downloading it directly from the Internet. For mobile devices you usually get your software from either the App Store (iPhones) or Play Store (Androids), and your chances of getting some malicious software is not as high as if you were to do it on your computer.

Android devices are known to not be as secure as Apple devices since they are more open to letting outside developers create apps for the Android operating system. Apple tends to keep their hardware and software more locked down, which makes it more secure. You should still be cautious when downloading apps for either one, though.

When downloading software from the Internet, where you get it from can make all the difference in the world. Let's say you wanted to buy a copy of Microsoft Office to install on your home computer. You can find this software many places, such as the Microsoft site or on Amazon, etc. If you purchase and download Office from one of these reputable sites, then you will most likely be okay. If you were to download Office from somewhere that might not seem so legitimate, you never know what you might end up with. It might be the wrong version, not come with an installation serial number\key, or may not even be Office at all! This might seem a little over-exaggerated, which it is, but I just want to point out that you shouldn't just download software from anywhere that is convenient or says they have the best deal.

*Free Software*
When it comes to downloading software, the ones that don't cost you anything are the ones to watch out for. The same thing applies here as it does with retail software. You need to consider where you are getting the software from before downloading it.

Many software providers will hide malicious software inside of their programs as a way to infect your computer without you knowing it. And by installing this software, *you* are the one who has actually infected your own computer! Sometimes when installing software you will get prompted to install additional software at the same time, and this is where they can get you as well if you are not paying attention.

Figure 9.23 shows one of these types of screens when installing some software called the Free YouTube Downloader. It is asking if you want to install the *Safe Saver* shopping software in addition to the YouTube Downloader software, but fortunately gives you the option to decline, which is a must in this situation. I have done this long enough to be able to tell when something doesn't look right, so if you can't tell for sure, then it's best to say no to stay safe.

Figure 9.23

Figures 9.24 and 9.25 show examples of legitimate software wanting to install additional software, which I always say no to as well because, for the most part, you don't want or need this extra software. If you are not paying attention and are just clicking *Next* through the screens, you might not see the checkbox and unintentionally install the extra software and then have to go and remove it later on.

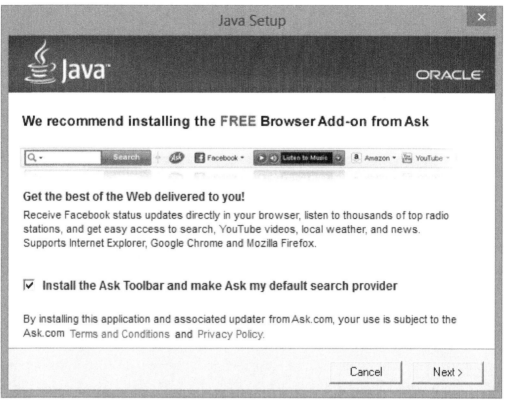

Figure 9.24

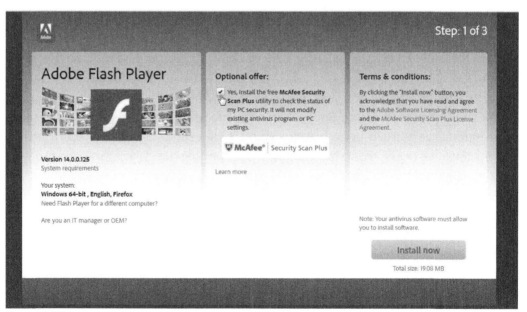

Figure 9.25

## Security Software

Now that I have most likely made you afraid to use the Internet, it's time to discuss some of the software out there that you can use to protect yourself from those who are out to get you. There are many options when it comes to this type of software, and some are free while others will cost you a little money. And believe it or not, there is also software out there that is designed to look like it's meant to protect you when, in fact, it's really only going to cause your computer harm.

You might have heard the terms "antivirus software" and also "antispyware" or "antimalware software" and are wondering what the difference is. Viruses, spyware, and malware all fall under the same category, spyware and malware basically being two different words for the same thing.

Viruses are designed to harm your computer and spread to other computers over networks and things such as shared USB drives. Spyware, on the other hand, is designed to steal information from you or find a way to make money off of you. You will find that spyware is more of an issue lately than viruses just because cybercriminals are more concerned with making money compared to breaking computers. With that being said, it's still necessary to have protection from both viruses and spyware\malware.

When it comes to antivirus software, there are many options out there to choose from with some being free and others costing money. I have found that the free ones actually do a good job, and there is not really a need to pay for the software. You might have to deal with some advertisements popping up or the software telling you that you can get advanced features with the pay-for version, but it's really not much of a hassle. If you are running Windows on your computer, then it will most likely come with built-in virus protection (depending on what version of Windows you are running). Macs don't really have a problem with viruses mainly because there are so many computers running Windows compared to Mac OS that hackers devote their time to Windows. You will hear people say that Macs are more secure, but they are susceptible to viruses as well. There just aren't as many out there.

Some of the free antivirus software that I have tried and like include the following.

- Sophos Home Antivirus
- AVG Free Antivirus
- Avast Free Antivirus
- Avira Free Antivirus

As for antispyware software, you also have many options of which some are free and some you have to pay for. Once again, there are some free options that work quite well. When shopping for antispyware software make sure you do your research and read real reviews so you don't end up installing the type that will actually cause more harm than good. Antivirus software generally runs in the background at all times and monitors everything you do, while antispyware software usually needs to be run manually to scan for issues. There are some products out there that will also monitor for spyware in real time. Here are a few antispyware products that I can recommend:

- Malwarebytes (They have a free version as well as a pay-for version that monitors in real time.)
- Spybot Search & Destroy 2 Anti Spyware
- Comodo Cleaning Essentials Security\Spyware Scanner
- Malwarebytes AdwCleaner Scanner

These types of products are also available for mobile devices, but are not needed as much as they are on computers (especially Windows), and you can get similar type apps for free. Once again, just be sure you are not installing something that will end up causing you problems rather than fixing problems.

 When downloading apps for your mobile device, be sure to look and see how many times the app has been downloaded. If it has several thousand or hundreds of thousands of downloads, then there is a better chance it is legitimate compared to one that only has a few hundred downloads. Be sure to read the reviews, too!

With a little caution and a lot of common sense, you can keep yourself pretty safe online and have fun discovering what the Internet has to offer. Just make sure you don't spend too much time online and not get anything else done!

## What's Next?

Now that you have read through this book and taken your online skills to the next level, you might be wondering what you should do next. Well, that depends on where you want to go. Are you happy with what you have learned, or do you want to further your knowledge on the Internet or even get into learning about networking or other, more advanced computer concepts?

If you do want to expand your knowledge, then you can look for some more advanced books or ones that cover the specific technology that interests you such as mastering Windows or even Google Apps. Focus on one subject at a time, then apply what you have learned to the next subject.

There are many great video resources as well, such as Pluralsight or CBT Nuggets, which offer online subscriptions to training videos of every type imaginable. YouTube is also a great source for training videos if you know what to search for.

If you are content in being a standalone Internet power user that knows more than your friends, then just keep on reading up on the technologies you want to learn, and you will soon become your friends and families go-to computer person, which may or may not be something you want!

Thanks for reading *The Internet Made Easy.* If you liked this title, please leave a review. Reviews help authors build exposure. Plus, I love hearing from my readers! You can also check out the other books in the Made Easy series for additional computer related information and training.

You should also check out my website at www.onlinecomputertips.com, as well as follow it on Facebook at https://www.facebook.com/OnlineComputerTips/ to find more information on all kinds of computer topics.

## About the Author

James Bernstein has been working with various companies in the IT field since 2000, managing technologies such as SAN and NAS storage, VMware, backups, Windows Servers, Active Directory, DNS, DHCP, Networking, Microsoft Office, Exchange, and more.

He has obtained certifications from Microsoft, VMware, CompTIA, ShoreTel, and SNIA, and continues to strive to learn new technologies to further his knowledge on a variety of subjects.

He is also the founder of the website onlinecomputertips.com, which offers its readers valuable information on topics such as Windows, networking, hardware, software, and troubleshooting. James writes much of the content himself, and adds new content on a regular basis. The site was started in 2005 and is still going strong today.